THE ART OF CLOSING THE SALE

The Key to Making More Money Faster
in the World of Professional Selling

Brian Tracy

THOMAS NELSON
Since 1798

NASHVILLE   DALLAS   MEXICO CITY   RIO DE JANEIRO   BEIJING

To my friend and business partner,
Victor Risling, the best salesman
and greatest closer I've ever seen.

Published in Nashville, Tennessee. Thomas Nelson is a registered trademark of Thomas Nelson, Inc.

Thomas Nelson, Inc. titles may be purchased in bulk for educational, business, fund-raising, or sales promotional use. For information, please e-mail SpecialMarkets@ThomasNelson.com.

Library of Congress Cataloging-in-Publication Data

Tracy, Brian.
  The art of closing the sale : the key to making more money faster in the world of professional selling / Brian Tracy.
     p. cm.
  ISBN: 978-0-7852-1429-8 (hardcover)
  ISBN: 978-0-7852-8913-5 (IE)
  1. Selling. I. Title.
  HF5438.25.T7117 2007
  658.85--dc22

                                                                2006034507

Printed in the United States of America
13 14 15 16 17 RRD 12 11 10 9 8

CONTENTS

INTRODUCTION

BREAKING THE SUCCESS
BARRIER IN SALES

WHEN I BEGAN SELLING, COLD-CALLING FROM OFFICE to office during the day, and from house to apartment during the evening, I was terrified of closing.

Every day, I would sally forth to sell, unafraid to get face-to-face with prospects and enthusiastically deliver my sales information. Then, at the end, I would choke up and ask hesitatingly, "What do you want to do now?"

Invariably, the prospect would say, "Well, leave it with me and let me think about it."

I learned later that the words, "Let me think it over" or "Let me think about it" are polite customer-speak for "Goodbye forever; we'll never meet again."

I convinced myself that people all over town were "thinking it over" and that my phone would soon fall off the hook with eager buyers. But no one ever called.

I finally realized that it was not the product, the price, the market, or the competition that was holding me back from making sales. It was me. More specifically, it was my fear of asking a closing question.

One day, I decided that I had had enough of frustration and failure. My very next call, when the prospect said, "Let me think about it; why don't you call me back," I said something that changed my life.

I replied, my heart in my throat, "I'm sorry, I don't make callbacks."

"Excuse me," he said, a bit surprised. "You don't make callbacks?"

"No," I said. "You know everything you need to know to make a decision right now. Why don't you just take it?"

He looked at me, then down at my brochure, and then looked up and said, "Well, if you don't make callbacks, I might as well take it."

He got out his checkbook, signed the order, paid me, and thanked me for coming. I walked out with the order in a mild state of shock. I had just experienced a major breakthrough.

I went next door, made my presentation to the decision-maker, and used the same words when he asked for time to think it over: "I don't make callbacks."

He said, "All right, then I'll take it now."

After my third sale in less than forty-five minutes, compared with my normal rate of three sales per week, I was walking on air! Within one month, I had broken every sales record for my company, been promoted to sales manager, and increased my income twenty times. I had thirty-two salespeople under me, all of whom I trained to ask for the order at the first meeting. Business boomed!

Over the years I have learned that knowledge of the key closing skills is essential to your making the kind of money you are truly capable of.

I have studied, practiced, and used countless sales-closing techniques, all included in this book, and trained more than 1,000,000 salespeople to be sales stars.

The biggest single obstacle to great success in selling is your ability to get a prospect to take action. The purpose of this book is to show you how to remove this obstacle so that you can make all the sales and all the money you want.

All top salespeople are good at closing. They know how to prospect professionally, identify needs, build trust, answer objections, and ask for the order in several different ways. They understand why prospects hesitate and delay, and they know how to structure their offerings to overcome these obstacles. As a result, they join the top 20 percent of salespeople who make all the money.

When I started out in selling, I got no training at all. I was given some brochures to read and told to "go out and talk to people." I was nervous about cold-calling and afraid of rejection, of which I got a lot. I trudged from office to office and from door to door, barely making enough to get by.

The Great Question

Then one day, I began asking, "Why is it that some sales-people are more successful than others?" This question changed my life.

From that day forward, I asked other salespeople for advice, especially on how to answer objections and close sales. I read every book I could find and practiced the best answers they contained. I listened to audio programs of top salespeople explaining their techniques. I attended sales seminars and sat up front.

Most of all, I took action on everything I learned. If it sounded good, I would go out immediately and try it on real, live prospects. I discovered later that this is the only way to learn, when there is a real possibility of succeeding or failing.

Above all, I learned how to ask for the order and to close the sale. I practiced every closing technique I found several times with hesitant prospects. Eventually I reached the point where I was completely unafraid to ask the prospect to make a buying decision. This skill quickly took me from rags to riches, from new salesperson to the top of every sales organization I ever worked for.

The Great Breakthrough

I later learned a remarkable thing: if you are completely fluent in closing and absolutely confident in your ability to ask for the order at the end of your sales presentation, you will be more aggressive about prospecting in the first place. You will have higher self-esteem and a better self-image. You will be more active each sales day, and you will even use your time better.

Because you *know* that you can close the sale, you will feel like a winner most of the time. This self-confidence will positively affect your prospects, making them even more likely to buy from you. Your whole sales career will move onto an upward spiral of increasing success.

The best news is that all sales skills, including closing, are learned and learnable. If you can drive a car, you can learn how to close the sale.

The best news is that all sales skills, including closing, are learned and *learnable*. If you can drive a car, you can learn how to close the sale. The only reason that you may be nervous about closing today is because you have not yet mastered the process. But once you learn to close, using these time-tested methods, you can use them over and over. As you do, you will get better and better.

In no time at all, you will be one of the most successful and highest-paid people in your field, and your future will be unlimited.

1

DEVELOPING A POWERFUL SALES PERSONALITY

*To be what we are, and to become what we are
capable of becoming, is the only real end of life.*

—Robert Louis Stevenson

BECOMING EXCELLENT IN CLOSING SALES IS AN INSIDE job. It begins within you. In sales, your personality is more important than your product knowledge. It is more important than your sales skills. It is more important than the product or service that you are selling. In fact, your personality determines fully 80 percent of your sales success.

This is easily proven by the fact that there are salespeople who can still achieve high sales volumes even with a highly competitive, expensive product in a depressed market.

1

At the same time, there are people with exclusive products in buoyant markets who are selling poorly.

Becoming Mentally Fit

Mental fitness is very similar to physical fitness in several ways. Physical fitness requires proper diet and exercise. Mental fitness requires a proper *mental* diet and regular practice. Become more mentally fit, and your happiness and sales volume will rise accordingly.

Top salespeople have high levels of self-confidence and self-esteem. Self-confidence is the natural growth of liking and respecting yourself. The better you feel about yourself, the more confidence you will have in prospecting, presenting, and closing sales.

Like and care about yourself, and you will genuinely like others and be more successful with them.

Without self-confidence, it is almost impossible to be successful in selling. If you lack confidence, you will come up with every excuse to avoid talking to prospects or taking any action where there is a possibility for failure or rejection.

Remember, the more you like yourself, the more you like others. You like other people; they will have confidence in you. The more confidence they have in you, the more likely that they will buy what you are selling.

We always feel better accepting the recommendation of someone whom we feel likes us than someone we are not sure about. We prefer to buy from people whom we feel care about us. Like and care about yourself, and you will genuinely like others and be more successful with them.

Take Charge of Your Life

Sometimes I ask my sales audiences, "How many people here are self-employed?"

About 10 or 15 percent of the audience raises their hands. Then I ask again, "How many people are *really* self-employed?"

One by one the audience realizes what I am getting at. One at a time they raise their hands. They suddenly realize that they are *all* self-employed.

The biggest mistake you can make is to ever think that you work for anyone but yourself. From the time you take your first job until the day you retire, you are self-employed. You are the *president* of your own entrepreneurial corporation, selling your services into the marketplace at the highest price possible. You have only one employee—yourself. Your job is to sell the highest quality and quantity of your services throughout your working life.

Top salespeople accept 100 percent responsibility for themselves and everything they do. They take full responsibility for their activities and for their results. They refuse to make excuses or blame others. They say no to criticizing and complaining. Top salespeople say, "If it's to be, it's up to me!"

View Yourself as Self-Employed

In a study done in New York some years ago, researchers found that the top 3 percent of people in every field looked upon themselves as self-employed. They treated the company as if it belonged to them personally. They saw themselves as being in charge of every aspect of their lives. They took everything that happened to their company personally, exactly as if they owned 100 percent of the stock.

The biggest mistake you can make is to ever think that you work for anyone but yourself. From the time you take your first job until the day you retire, you are self-employed.

The sales manager of a Fortune 500 company once told me an interesting story. He said that he was with his top salesman, negotiating the final terms and conditions of a $200 million contract with a major client. During a break, the client pulled him aside and asked, referring to the salesman, "That man owns your company, doesn't he?"

The sales manager, knowing the salesman, was a bit surprised. He said, "What makes you say that?"

"Well," the client said, "in all my meetings with him, he constantly refers to the company as 'my company' and 'my people,' 'my contract' and so on. He sounds like he actually owns the whole company. Is that true?"

My friend, the sales manager, smiled and said, "Yes, in a way he does."

You Are the Boss

As the president of your own personal services corporation, you are 100 percent in charge of everything that happens to your business. You are in command of training and development, and of continually upgrading your skills. You are in control of sales and marketing, production and quality control, and personal organization and efficiency. You are the boss.

It is absolutely amazing how many people see themselves passively rather than actively. Instead of taking charge of their lives and changing things they don't like, they wait passively for the company to come along and do it for them. The great majority of adults do not invest in their own personal and professional development. They do not read, listen to audio programs, or attend courses. They expect the company to do this for them, not only to pay for it, but also to give them the time off to upgrade their skills so *they* can earn more money. Go figure.

Be Aggressive About Learning

Take all the training you can get. Use every job you have as an opportunity to learn more skills that you can use for the rest of your life. Be aggressive about upgrading your knowledge. If your company offers any training opportunities, accept them immediately. Don't delay. Every new skill you learn is an investment in your own future.

Everything you have in your life today is a result of your own choices up to now. Your current situation is a result of both your actions and your *inactions* in the past. The amount you earn today is due to both what you have done and what you have failed to do. Sometimes the things you fail to do, like completing your education or improving your skills once you start work, have a greater impact on your future than the things that you actually do.

Winners Versus Losers

The difference between winners and losers in this area is quite clear. Winners always accept responsibility themselves for the consequences of their actions. Losers never do but instead always have some kind of explanation for why they are doing poorly.

Winners are solution oriented. They are always looking for ways to solve the problems and deal with the challenges they face each day.

Losers have a disease called excuse-itis, which we define as "an inflammation of the excuse-making gland." It is invariably *fatal* to success. Once a person is infected with excuse-itis, instead of making progress, he makes excuses for every difficulty in his life.

Winners are different. Winners are solution oriented. They are always looking for ways to solve the problems and deal with the challenges they face each day. They continually try new things. If one thing doesn't work, they try something else. They never consider the possibility of failure.

Be Prepared to Work Hard

A major difference between successful salespeople and average salespeople is that successful salespeople work much *harder* than the average. In author Thomas Stanley's research for his book *The Millionaire Next Door*, 85 percent of the self-made millionaires he interviewed attributed their success to "hard, hard work."

Over and over, when successful people are questioned, in any area of life, they say things like, "I was no smarter than other people, but I was willing to work harder than they were."

Average people *want* to work hard. They *intend* to work hard. They are planning to work hard—sometime in the future. They even claim that they work hard and complain about how diligently they work, but they don't really work very hard at all.

Don't Waste Time

The average salesperson today wastes a full 50 percent of his or her working time. According to the research, he comes in a little later, works a little slower, and leaves a little earlier. He spends most of his working time in idle chitchat with coworkers, personal business, reading the paper, drinking coffee, and surfing the Internet.

Winners are different. They arrive a little earlier, work a little harder, and stay a little later. They work through their lunch hours and coffee breaks. They work in the evenings and prepare in the mornings. They make every minute count.

Pay the Price in Advance

H. L. Hunt, owner of more than two hundred companies and at one time the richest man in the world, was once asked on a radio interview for his "secret of success." He replied,

I have started and built hundreds of companies. In 50 years of experience, I have found that there are only two things necessary for success.

First, decide exactly what you want. Most people never do this. Second, determine the price that you are going to have to pay to get what you want, and then resolve to pay that price.

Top salespeople are absolutely determined to succeed, and they are willing to pay the price, in advance.

Ambition and Desire

Ambition and desire are the foundation qualities of all great achievement. As it turns out, top salespeople have above-average ambition and desire to sell.

Top salespeople have a burning commitment and an

intense desire to be successful. They will not let anything stop them. To put it another way, they are "hungry."

Average salespeople think in terms of making just enough money to pay their bills. They think about getting one more sale so they can get through one more month. They don't believe in putting in the extra efforts that are essential for great success.

Make the Extra Effort

Some time ago, a large insurance company had a sales competition each year in November. Everyone who hit the target, which was about 35 percent above their monthly average for the year, received two weeks' vacation in the Caribbean as a bonus.

Each November, during the contest period, the sales force came alive. They worked day and night to qualify for those two weeks in the sun. Salespeople who had average sales throughout the year became superstars for that thirty-day period.

One year, the insurance company went back and reviewed the sales of each person who qualified every November. They made a startling discovery: the average salesperson was selling *three* policies a week during the year. But in the contest period, they increased their sales to an average of *four* policies a week. By starting a little earlier and working a little harder, those who qualified for the Caribbean vacation were selling one extra policy during the forty- to fifty-hour week.

The managers sat down with their salespeople and pointed out that if they put in a little extra effort throughout the year, they could be in that prizewinning, high-income category all year long, instead of just once a year. They showed how this would translate into income over a forty-year career.

If a person started selling when she was twenty-five and sold until she was sixty-five, and if the average salesperson made four sales per week rather than three, this would translate into ten extra years of income. In other words, a salesperson could achieve the same amount of income in thirty years that she would in forty years. And she would have the money ten years earlier.

No Ambition, No Hope

Sometimes people approach me at my seminars and tell me that they have no ambition. They say they are quite content at their level of income. They make enough to pay their bills and stay out of debt. They ask me what I can do for them if they lack an all-consuming desire to accomplish more than they are already achieving.

Reluctantly, I tell them that there is really no hope for them if they have no ambition. If they don't have the desire themselves to be more and do better than they are today, there is nothing that anyone else can do for them. I tell them, "Some people are born to be followers, and some people are born to be leaders, and I have to assume that you were born to be a follower." I have never met anyone who particularly likes this response. Too bad. Ambition is *essential* for great success.

Develop Empathy and Understanding

Top salespeople also have high levels of *empathy*, i.e., they really care about their customers. Ambition, the desire to achieve, combined with empathy, the genuine caring for the well-being of your customers, are the twin keys to top sales performance.

Daniel Goleman, author of *Emotional Intelligence,* says that EQ or *emotional quotient* is more important than IQ, *intelligence quotient*, for success. He defines emotional intelligence as the ability to get along well with a large number of other people and to be sensitive to their thoughts, feelings, and moods. He concludes that empathy is the most important of all qualities for building and maintaining high-quality relationships with other people, both at home and at work.

You have empathy for your customers when you make every effort to understand them, to "walk a mile in their shoes." A person with *sympathy* may feel sorry for another person, but he looks at him from the *outside.* A person with *empathy* makes every effort to get *inside* the mind and heart of the customer and to understand his situation and needs. There is an old saying, "If you can see Joe Jones through Joe Jones's eyes, you can sell Joe Jones what Joe Jones buys."

THINK LONG TERM

Empathy requires the development of *long-time perspective.* Average salespeople think primarily in terms of making a sale right now, with little concern for long-term relationships or the future. Top salespeople, on the other hand, think about the second and third sales to this customer while still talking to him about the *first* sale. Further, they imagine selling to this customer twenty years from now. Everything they do in their dealings with this customer today is with a view to the long term. As a result, they are far more empathetic in the short term than average salespeople.

> Top salespeople think about the second and third sales to this customer while still talking to him about the first sale. Further, they imagine selling to this customer twenty years from now.

Poor salespeople look upon every transaction as an opportunity to make a sale and then get out. Peak-performance salespeople do not think in terms of closing sales as much as they think in terms of opening long-term customer relationships.

THE IDEAL COMBINATION

A balance between ambition and empathy seems to be the ideal combination for long-term sales success. If a salesperson is too ambitious, he will not care that much for the customer, and the customer will sense this. If a salesperson is too empathetic, he will not be assertive enough to ask for the sale. Balance is essential.

Customers today are smarter than they have ever been in history, and they are getting smarter every day. They are the most sophisticated, knowledgeable, demanding, and even disloyal consumers of all time.

Today's customer has had so much experience with so many salespeople that she can see through a salesperson like seeing through plastic wrap. If the salesperson is not seriously concerned about her well-being, she perceives it immediately. She doesn't have to think about it. She knows in a few minutes whether the salesperson is selling just for himself, or if he is genuinely concerned about the customer's interest.

ASK GOOD QUESTIONS AND LISTEN CAREFULLY

The very best way to express and practice empathy with a customer, or with anyone else, is to ask questions and listen intently to the answers. Dominate the listening, rather than the talking. As Stephen Covey says, "Seek first to understand, then to be understood." The more time you invest in understanding your customer's situation, the more empathy you will naturally have for him or her and the more probable it is that you will make the sale in the end.

Keep On Keeping On

Top salespeople possess above average willpower and determination to succeed. They have the ability to keep on keeping on, even in the face of disappointments and setbacks. They are willing to pay the price of success in advance.

They are eager to work hard. They are prepared to go the extra mile. They know that "there are never any traffic jams on the extra mile."

The highest-paid salespeople realize that every bit of success that they aspire to must be paid in full, *in advance*. There is no such thing as *something for nothing*, no fast, easy way to be successful. The only way to get to the top is through hard, hard work, sustained over a long period of time.

> *The highest-paid salespeople realize that every bit of success that they aspire to must be paid in full, in advance. There is no such thing as something for nothing, no fast, easy way to be successful*

Many salespeople are led astray by stories of people who have gotten into a particular field or made a specific investment and earned a lot of money in a short period of time. These cases are very rare, and in most cases, the people who made a lot of money quickly lost it just as quickly. As they say, "Easy come, easy go."

The Highest-Income Years

Most people make their highest incomes after the fortieth or forty-fifth year of their lives. Some do it faster, but the vast majority of individuals only develop the knowledge and experience necessary to achieve high earnings a bit later in life. The average forty-year-old in the United States has a net worth of $1,010. One-third of baby boomers, who will be retiring in the next few years, are broke. They have nothing saved up at all. This is all too common.

Be willing to pay the price in terms of ambition, desire, hard work, and determination, extended over a long period of time, to achieve the success that you desire. As you practice what you learn in this book, you will move ahead faster than you ever imagined possible.

Get Rich Slowly but Surely

Henry Ford once said, "The two most important qualities for success in business are *patience* and *foresight*, and the man who lacks patience is not cut out for success in competitive enterprise." There is no fast, effortless way to make money. Get-rich-quick schemes only work for the person selling them. Don't waste a minute of your life trying to cut corners or create financial shortcuts. Chasing the will-o'-the-wisp of the quick buck is the surest way to destroy your character and undermine your career.

The worst thing that can happen to a salesperson is to make a lot of money during an economic boom, especially at the beginning of his career. As a result, he gets the idea that making money is easy. For the rest of his life, then, he searches for the next opportunity to make easy money. He seldom succeeds. Worse, this early success causes him never to settle down to do the hard work and make the necessary sacrifices to achieve enduring success. Soon he stops believing in himself, and to stop believing is to fail.

Believe in Yourself and What You Are Selling

Top salespeople have high levels of belief in themselves. They also believe in their companies *and* their product or service's value to the customer.

There seems to be a direct relationship between how much you believe in your product or service and how easily you can convince a customer to believe in it. Your customer can never believe in your product any more than you do. As William James of Harvard said, "Belief creates the actual fact."

This is why it is so important for you to sell something that you believe in, something that you consider good for your customer to own or use. Everyone has experienced having to sell something that he or she didn't think was particularly good. If you have this feeling, you will never be successful in a competitive market. If you cannot put your whole heart into what you are selling, you will not sell very much of it.

THE FAILURE FORMULA

Salespeople approach me continually, saying, "I don't really like this product [or this company, or the people I work with, or the people I have to sell to], but I want to be successful at selling it. What advice can you give me?"

I cannot help them. If you don't *love* your product and really believe in it, you cannot possibly be successful selling it. The competition is too great. If you don't respect your company and your boss, and you don't like your customers, you don't stand a chance against a sales professional who does.

In fact, you cannot even be *lukewarm* about your product and be successful in a competitive market. You have to believe that your product is absolutely *excellent*. You also have to believe that your customer can really benefit from using it. If you don't believe these things deep in your heart, you will never convince others that they should have it.

Do What You Love to Do

One of the secrets of success in selling is for you to do what you love to do. Top salespeople love what they are selling. They believe in it passionately. They will defend it and argue over it. They will talk about it day and night. When they go to bed, they think about their product. When they wake up in the morning, they can hardly wait to talk to prospects about it.

Look at the top salespeople in the very best companies, and you'll find that these people are *fanatical* about their

> *"When you get into this business, you will make a living. But when the business gets into you, you will make a great life." Truer words were never spoken.*

products and services. That is why they sell so much. One of my top salesmen once said, "When you get into this business, you will make a living. But when the business gets into you, you will make a great life." Truer words were never spoken.

Keep Your Word

Top-selling salespeople are impeccably honest with themselves and with others. There is no substitute for honesty in selling. Earl Nightingale once said, "If honesty did not exist, it would have to be invented as the surest way of getting rich."

Ralph Waldo Emerson wrote, "Guard your integrity as a sacred thing." You must be perfectly honest with yourself in all things. Live in truth with yourself and others. Be completely truthful in terms of the work that you have to do to achieve the rewards that you want to enjoy.

The average person is built like a human lie detector. Because he has had so many experiences with half-honest or dishonest people, the typical consumer can pick up insincerity or falsehood across a crowded room. Everyone can. The worst fool in the world is the one who thinks he can fool someone else.

THE CRITICAL DIFFERENCE

A national trade organization to which I belong commissioned a study to find out why customers bought from one person or company and not from another, even though the products were similar. After investing $50,000 interviewing customers, they arrived at a simple conclusion: people bought from one person over another because they *trusted* that person more. The word *trust* was defined as "feeling the salesperson would follow through on his commitments and fulfill his promises."

Tell the Truth

It is crucial that you never say your product will do anything that it will *not do*. Never make false claims. Never even exaggerate. In fact, one of the most helpful things you can do to establish your credibility is to point out where your product is weak in comparison with that of your competitors.

Put These Qualities Together

The top salesperson, because he has a *combination* of all these qualities, has a natural ability to turn strangers into friends wherever he goes. When you are completely honest with yourself and you practice the quality of empathy with others, you like yourself more, and your customers will, in turn, like and accept you.

There is a 1:1 relationship between being and becoming an excellent person and high levels of self-esteem. The rule is that you can never like or love anyone else more than you like yourself. So don't expect anyone else to like you more than you like yourself. How you feel about yourself is the single most important determinant of the quality of all your relationships, both personal and business.

Choosing the Right Product for You

Choosing the product or service to sell is very much like dating or getting married. There has to be the right chemistry, or it won't work. It has to be a product or service that you like, enjoy, and feel is good for others. It must be compatible with your personality.

Each person is different. Sometimes an excellent salesperson will do poorly because she is selling the wrong product for her. This does not mean there is something wrong with the product or service. It simply means that the salesperson and the product are *incompatible*.

> *Choosing the product or service to sell is very much like dating or getting married. There has to be the right chemistry, or it won't work.*

There are two types of products, tangible and intangible. Some people are capable of selling tangible products, and some are capable of selling intangible products. If you can sell the one, you probably cannot sell the other.

A TANGIBLE PRODUCT

A tangible product is something you can touch, taste, feel, hold, demonstrate, and try out. Examples include a car, a boat, office equipment, furniture, decorations, computers, watches, or tools. If you are the kind of person who likes tangible products, you will only be successful when you are selling them. You can relate to them and enjoy them. You feel happy when you are talking about them, describing them, and selling them to others. You will never be successful or happy selling an intangible product.

An Intangible Product or Service

An intangible product, on the other hand, is something that you *cannot* touch or taste. Intangible products are usually *ideas* of some kind. For example, investments are an idea. Insurance is an idea. Education and training products and services are ideas. Even real estate as an investment is an idea based on concepts and numbers more than it is a tangible product.

If you are the kind of person who loves ideas and concepts, you will only be content selling some kind of intangible product.

Trust Your Intuition

The best way to ascertain which type of salesperson you are is to ask yourself, *am I interested in concrete products and things, or in the world of ideas?* Do you like to work with your hands and deal with products that you can touch and feel? Or you do like philosophy, psychology, and metaphysics? If you enjoy discussing politics and religion or your interests are drawn to concepts, you will be happiest selling intangible services. If your major interest is in solid things like houses, cars, clothes, and computers, then you should sell tangibles.

If you ever get into a field and feel uncomfortable selling a particular product or service, this is an indication that you may be selling the wrong product for your individual personality. When you are selling the right thing for you, you will become involved *emotionally*. It will excite you and interest you. It will absorb your attention. You will like to think about and discuss it with others. But if your heart is not in what you are selling, you may be selling the wrong thing for you.

THE KEY TO SUCCESS

To be successful in selling, you must actually love your product and be excited about what it can do to improve the life or work of your customers. You will only be fruitful when you believe that what you are selling is a great product or service in comparison with everything else that is on the market.

The "acid test" of whether or not you are selling the right product for you is your level of *enthusiasm* about it. Since enthusiasm is an emotion that comes from within, it can only be triggered when what you are doing on the outside is in harmony with what you feel on the inside. If you are not enthusiastic about what you are doing, it is obviously the wrong thing for you.

Admire Successful People

Perhaps the most common emotions of poor performers are *envy* and *resentment*. They are jealous of other people's success. They seek every opportunity to criticize and complain about high-performance people, usually behind their backs. Fortunately, their negative attitude has no effect on these high achievers. But it dooms these underachievers to personal failure throughout their careers.

Always *admire* the top people in your field. Speak positively about them. Look up to them, and use them as your role models. Try to emulate them in every way possible. Be happy for their success. Keep reminding yourself that anything that they have accomplished, you can accomplish as well. Be grateful that there are people ahead of you and making more money than you, because this is proof that you can achieve the same goals. Always want for others what you want for yourself.

Program Yourself for Success

When you admire and look up to other successful people, you program your subconscious mind to do and say exactly the same things that they do. And when you program your subconscious mind for achievement, it will find ways to help you. It will give you inspiration and energy to move you toward your goals. It will attract people and ideas into your life. Your subconscious mind will give you answers to solve your problems, and strategies to achieve your goals. It is the most powerful force in the world, and you can use it any way you want.

Your subconscious mind . . . is the most powerful force in the world, and you can use it any way you want.

Confidently Expect to Succeed

In more than fifty years of motivational research, psychologists have found that an attitude of *confident expectations* seems to go hand in hand with great success in every area. If you confidently expect to succeed, in advance, you will be optimistic. This optimism has an effect on everyone around you, making them respond more positively toward you and your offerings.

The law of expectations says, "Whatever you expect, with confidence, becomes your own self-fulfilling prophecy." If you expect to succeed, you will succeed. If you expect to be popular wherever you go, you will be popular. If you expect to have a good time at a party, you will have a good time. Your expectations will become your realities.

Your expectations exert an inordinate influence on other people. If you confidently expect to sell to a prospect, this expectation is picked up by the subconscious mind of the prospect. In a very positive way, your expectations enable you to influence the prospect into making a buying decision that is good for both of you.

RESOLVE TO EXPECT THE BEST

One of the greatest obstacles to selling is *negative expectations*. These occur when the salesperson, as a result of attitude or previous experience, does not expect to be successful. He unconsciously manufactures these negative expectations in advance, and when he goes in to see the prospect, he has already convinced himself that he is wasting his time. The prospect picks up on this feeling of negative expectation and responds negatively to the offering.

Your expectations, positive or negative, are completely

under your own control. They can help you or hurt you. And good or bad, they influence the behavior of those around you. Be sure that you manufacture and maintain only positive expectations in everything you do.

Confidently Ignore Customer Skepticism

Virtually all customers are hesitant about buying. They are skeptical. They have been burned many times by salespeople in the past. As a result, they give a lot of knee-jerk objections and reasons for not buying. "I'm not interested." "I don't have the money." "Business is slow right now." "Let me think it over." "I need to talk to someone else." "Leave me something to look at," and so on. But none of these are real reasons for not buying. They are normal and automatic responses to any sales offering.

However, if you confidently expect to sell, and take no note of these objections, the customer eventually begins to relax and come around. Many an uncertain buyer has been completely turned around by the positive attitude and confident expectations of the salesperson.

The salesperson simply ignored the initial sales resistance and kept on talking, asking questions, and listening. Eventually, the customer's resistance broke down, and he decided to buy.

When you have been sold by a professional salesperson, you stay sold. You actually enjoy the experience. You don't experience buyer's remorse. You are happy that you bought the product or service, and you are eager to get it and begin using and enjoying it. And the more confident and positive the salesperson, the more satisfied you are with the buying experience. This should be your goal with each of your customers as well.

Change Your Thinking, Change Your Life

The law of correspondence says that "your outer world is a mirror of your inner world." In other words, everything that happens to you on the outside is a *reflection* of what is going on with you on the inside. If you want to change or improve any part of your sales or personal life, you have to begin by changing yourself on the inside. Everything we have been talking about so far has revolved around making these inner changes in a positive and constructive way.

Feed Your Mind with Mental Protein

Make the decision today to read in your field for thirty to sixty minutes each day. Like any professional, develop your own library of sales books. Each morning, instead of reading the newspaper or watching television, invest thirty to sixty minutes reading something on sales that will help you to perform better during the day.

Henry Ward Beecher once said, "The first hour is the rudder of the day." What you put into your mind in the first hour sets the tone of your mind for the rest of the day. If you feed your mind with something positive, educational, and uplifting in the first hour, you will perform better all day long. You will be more cheerful, relaxed, and self-assured. You will also be more resilient and will bounce back faster from rejection and disappointment.

Get up every morning two hours before your first appointment. If you have to be at work at 8:00 AM, get up at 6:00, spend an hour reading, and

All top people arise early and get going immediately. Average folks rise at the last possible minute, run around in circles, and then dash off for the office with no time for thinking or preparation.

then get ready for your day. All top people arise early and get going immediately. Average folks rise at the last possible minute, run around in circles, and then dash off for the office with no time for thinking or preparation.

BECOME A WELL-READ PROFESSIONAL

By getting up in the morning and reading a half hour to an hour in sales, you will find yourself reading about one sales book per week. This will translate into about fifty books per year. Fifty books per year multiplied by ten years will come to a total of five hundred books. Do you think this would have any effect on your sales results or your income?

The fact is that when you discipline yourself to read thirty to sixty minutes each day in your field, you will soon become one of the most knowledgeable, skilled, and highest-paid people in sales. By reading the very best books written by top salespeople over the years, you will learn ideas, insights, strategies, and techniques to help you make more sales faster than you could ever imagine.

Which books should you read? Don't worry. By the law of attraction, you will be drawn to exactly the right books at exactly the right time for you. As you build your sales library and read from it each morning, you will step on the accelerator of your own career. You will move faster and more confidently toward sales success. Your income will double and triple faster than you ever thought possible.

TRIPLE YOUR INCOME?

Not long ago, a young man, twenty years old, came to one of my public sales seminars. His name was Bob. He had long, unkempt hair, was poorly dressed, and had a negative attitude. During the seminar, I explained the importance of reading thirty to sixty minutes each morning. He sat in the back all day, taking notes, and left at the end of the day without saying anything to me.

About two months later, I got a phone call from his uncle. It turned out that Bob came from a broken family, was a high-school dropout, and had experienced some minor problems with the law. Finally, his uncle and aunt had taken him in. He was unemployed, had no ambition, and sat around watching TV most of the day. Ultimately, the uncle laid down the law and insisted that Bob get a job, any job, rather than continue to sit around the house.

A SLOW START IN SALES

Reluctantly, Bob went out and got a job in straight-commission selling, from house to house and business to business. As you can imagine, he did poorly. He made very few sales and very little money. But he had to keep this job in order to continue living with his uncle and aunt.

One day, the uncle saw the advertisement for my seminar in the paper and in desperation decided to send his nephew. Bob did not want to go. He only went because his uncle paid for it, drove him to the seminar, and picked him up afterward.

In the two months following the seminar, however, a miracle had taken place. The first thing Bob did when he got home was buy a book on selling. He then began getting up each morning and reading for thirty minutes before he went to his sales job. Within a week, he was reading an hour per day. Soon he was getting up at 5:00 AM and reading for two hours before he went off to work. In no time at all, his sales took off. Then they exploded. He started breaking sales records. And the more he sold, the more confident and enthusiastic he became.

A SUPERSTAR SALESPERSON

All by himself, he began to make changes in his physical appearance. He had his hair cut and groomed neatly. He bought new clothes so he looked like a professional. The other salespeople in his company began looking up to him and asking him for advice.

Six weeks after my course, they made him a sales manager

and put him in charge of a small territory. Two months after my course, he went with his uncle and bought his first car. He had tripled and quadrupled his income and completely changed his personality.

His uncle told me that Bob attributed all of his success to having been *forced* to go to my seminar. He said the most important thing he learned was the value of reading in sales for at least an hour every morning before starting out. It transformed his life.

Simple but Powerful

The average adult reads less than one book a year. Many salespeople do not read *at all* in the field of selling. In fact, a whopping 90 percent of sales books are bought by customers who are *not* in the sales profession. But whenever I talk with *top* salespeople about the importance of reading, I am always amazed to learn how many books they have read and are reading at the present time. They sound like sales libraries, rattling off titles, authors, and concepts from their libraries of sales books.

When you begin to read one book per week, fifty books a year, you will separate yourself completely from the ranks of average salespeople. You will put yourself onto the fast track and begin making more sales than you ever dreamed. Try it and prove it for yourself.

It is said that "reading is to the mind as exercise is to the body." The more you read, the sharper and more alert you become. When you read *more* in selling, you learn *more* new ideas to sell *more* of your products *more* effectively. The more you read, the faster you move to the top of your field.

SELECTING TOP SALESPEOPLE

One of my clients is a sales manager with thirty-two salespeople selling products in a very competitive industry. Yet the salespeople in his company earn an average of three times as much as those of his competitors who sell similar products. Because of this, everyone wants to work for him. Salespeople from other companies are continually applying to him for sales jobs.

He told me that he had developed a very simple way to sort out winners from losers in selling. When he sat down to interview a prospective salesperson, he would say, "Thank you for coming in. Before we begin, let me ask you a question. What are some of your favorite books and audio programs on sales in your personal development library?" Then he waits.

If the prospective salesperson hesitates or says, "I don't really have any," my friend stands up, takes her by the arm, and shows her the door.

If the prospective salesperson can quickly give the names of books and audio programs that he reads and listens to, he almost always gets the job.

A VALID TEST FOR PREDICTING SUCCESS

What this manager had learned was that a salesperson who was not personally committed to becoming better by investing her own money in books and audio programs would never be successful in a competitive market. It was a waste of time to hire and attempt to train such a person. He had learned from experience to only hire people who were already committed to their own personal and professional self-development programs. These were the people who very soon became sales superstars and earned three times as much as their competitors in rival companies.

> *"If you are not continually learning and upgrading your skills, somewhere, someone else is, and when you meet that person, you will lose."*
> —*Reed Buckley*

It would be the same as an athlete who is overweight, unfit, smokes, eats too much, and doesn't train trying to compete in any sport. No matter how nice or sincere a person he is or how much he desires to win, he doesn't have a chance against well-trained, determined competition.

Author Reed Buckley once said, "If you are not continually learning and upgrading your skills, somewhere, someone else is, and when you meet that person, you will lose."

Listen to Audio Programs

Business speaker Nick Carter once said, "Audio learning is the greatest breakthrough in education since the invention of the printing press."

When I started off in sales, frustrated and unhappy, working long hours and getting few results, someone introduced me to audio learning. It changed my life. Even now, after all these years, I still remember the wonderful experience of listening to top salespeople on audio sharing their experiences and explaining their methods. Some of them are still with me today.

Back when the personal computer was new, there was the term *GIGO*, which means "garbage in, garbage out." These letters could also stand for "good in, good out." When you

You can get the equivalent of a full-time university education each year just by listening to educational audio programs as you drive from place to place.

continually feed your mind with audio learning as you travel from call to call, you program yourself at a deep level to say and do what the winners would do during a sales situation.

TURN TRAVELING TIME INTO LEARNING TIME

The average sales professional drives about 25,000 miles per year. This means that, allowing for traffic, the average salesperson sits behind the wheel about 1,000 hours per year. This is the equivalent of six months of forty-hour weeks, or two university semesters.

The University of California released a study recently that showed that you can get the equivalent of a full-time university education each year just by listening to educational audio programs as you drive from place to place.

From this day forward, turn your car into a "classroom on

wheels." As Zig Ziglar says, "Enroll in Automobile University and attend full time for the rest of your career."

By turning your car into a "learning machine," you will be amazed at the enormous number of great ideas you will hear each week, each month, and each year.

CONDENSED KNOWLEDGE

A good audio learning program contains the best ideas of ten, twenty, and even fifty books. To buy and read these books would cost you hundreds of dollars and take hundreds of hours. Instead, you can get the distilled essence of the best thinkers in your field by simply listening to audio programs as you drive around.

Not only that, you can stop the audio program when you come to a particularly good idea and take some time to think about how you could use it in your sales work. You can repeat an audio program and listen to it several times. By listening to such programs, you keep your mind awake and alert throughout the sales day. Like a star athlete, when you arrive to call on a prospect, you will be attentive and prepared to perform at your best.

MAKE EVERY MINUTE COUNT

The great tragedy is that mediocre salespeople waste this precious learning time. They drive around listening to the radio or to music in their cars. They miss one of the great learning opportunities that is available to professional salespeople.

It is said that radio is "chewing gum for the ears." For the salesperson, listening to the radio is the equivalent of an athlete's dieting on candy and soft drinks. He loses his focus. He gets distracted by what's on the air. Instead of thinking about how to sell more effectively, his mental powers are weakened. He loses his "edge." Don't let this happen to you.

Do What the Top People Do

The highest-paid salespeople I know listen to audio programs all the time. Their cars are mobile "classrooms." They usually carry several different audio programs and alternate them based on what they feel they need to learn the most at that moment. The best salespeople don't even know if their radios work, because they never turn them on.

Are You Serious?

If a person in the competitive field of sales insists on listening to the radio as she drives around, it is an indication that she is simply not serious about her success. I have worked with countless sales professionals who have struggled for years at low levels of income, and then, as the result of listening to one audio program (often one of mine), their incomes have doubled and tripled, sometimes in as little as thirty days.

Wouldn't it be a tragedy if the only thing holding you back from earning two or three times as much as you are earning today was the information contained in a single audio program?

The Magic Questions

There are two great questions that you can use to accelerate your growth toward high income in sales. These are two of the best questions that I have ever learned. I have used them over the years, and they have been responsible for making or saving me many thousands of dollars.

The first question to ask yourself after each sales call is, *what did I do right?*

This question keeps you focused on the best parts of your performance. Even if the sales call was a complete failure, there were certain things that you did correctly. It is important that you identify the best parts of your performance so you do not throw out the baby with the bathwater.

You could write down:

"I was thoroughly prepared."

"I researched the client in advance."

"I was punctual for my appointment."

"I was well dressed and groomed."

"I asked questions and listened carefully before speaking."

"I made a complete presentation."

"I asked for the order twice," and so on.

By asking the question, *what did I do right?* you keep yourself continually focused on the best elements of your sales activities. By reviewing these activities immediately after a sales call, you program them into your subconscious and create a predisposition to repeat these positive behaviors at your next sales call.

Focus on Improvement

The second question you must ask yourself is, *what would I do differently?*

This question forces you to think about the positive things that you could do to improve your performance in a similar situation. Even if the sales call has been completely successful, there were still things that you could do differently in the future to make it even better.

The advantage of these two questions is that the answers to both of them are *positive*. Force yourself to review and mentally rehearse the very greatest ingredients of your performance. Then, the next time you are in a similar situation, your subconscious mind will pass them back up to you and make them available to you for the sales call.

Program Yourself Positively

Average salespeople have a tendency to ask the wrong questions. Instead of asking themselves, *what did I do right?* they ask themselves, *what did I do wrong?* Rather than focusing on the best components of their performance, they focus on the *worst*. This simply programs them to repeat those mistakes at the next sales call. "What would I do differently?" is superior to "What mistakes did I make?" Dwell on your mistakes and shortcomings, and you can be certain you will see them again.

Successful people continually recall their very best sales calls. They review and rehearse the best things that they said and did with the customer. As a result, they continually program high performance into their subconscious minds.

They then repeat their very best performances over and over again in subsequent sales calls.

The Power of Suggestion

The *power of suggestion* exerts a strong influence on you throughout your day, and throughout your life. One of the keys to success is to take complete control of the suggestive influences that you allow to reach your conscious and subconscious minds. You must make every effort to ensure that the mental influences around you are as positive as possible, just as you would only eat really healthy foods if you wanted to feel the best about yourself physically.

You are positively or negatively influenced by every sight, sound, thought, experience, and person in your world. If you watch negative or violent television programs, it affects you at an unconscious level and makes you a more negative person. If you listen to useless babble on the radio, it clogs up your mind as sludge clogs up a drain and makes you less effective. If you read unconstructive material in books, magazines, or newspapers, it fills your mind with mental garbage that can demotivate you and make you more easily discouraged.

GET AROUND THE RIGHT PEOPLE

Perhaps the most important part of your suggestive environment is the set of people with whom you associate most of the time. Dr. David McClelland of Harvard, in his book

The Achieving Society, found that a negative "reference group" was enough in itself to condemn a person to lifelong failure.

Your reference group consists of the people around you, the people with whom you associate, and the people with whom you identify. Your most important reference group, in forming your personality, is your family. If your parents were disapproving and critical, this can affect you all your life. Whether your brothers and sisters were helpful or hurtful can have an effect on you for many years. As you grow up, your friends at school, your teachers, teammates, and other associates exert an inordinate influence on your thinking and your emotions.

FLY WITH THE EAGLES

As an adult, you must choose your friends and associates with care. As Zig Ziglar says, "You cannot fly with the eagles if you continue to scratch with the turkeys." Get around positive people. Associate with those who are going somewhere with their lives. Socialize with folks who are positive and who have goals for themselves and their work. Only spend time with people who have virtues that you admire and want to emulate yourself.

Meanwhile, get away from negative people. Avoid those who complain and criticize much of the time. Especially avoid joining in when people start complaining about their work or about other successful people. This is a sort of "loser slime" that gets all over you and can ruin all of your chances for success.

KEEP YOUR OWN COMPANY

Remember the old sayings "Like attracts like" and "Birds of a feather flock together"? Top salespeople tend to be loners. This does not mean that they are "*a*loners." It simply means that they are selective about the people with whom they spend time. They do not drink coffee with whoever is sitting there or go out for lunch with whoever is standing at the door. Instead, they deliberately choose their companions. They either spend their time by themselves or with those people whose company is valuable and worthwhile to them. You must do the same.

The 100-Call Method

Here is a powerful way to put all these ideas to work. It is called the "100-call method." Whenever I have started a new sales job, I have made it a point to hit the ground running. I set a goal to make 100 face-to-face calls in the shortest period of time possible. From that moment on, I get up early, prepare thoroughly, and then work steadily all day long, often cold-calling, to complete my 100-call goal.

Don't worry about whether or not you sell anything during these 100 calls. Put the idea of selling aside for now and just concentrate on getting face-to-face with 100 people and telling them about your product or service. Two wonderful things will happen during this time. First of all, by dedicating yourself to seeing 100 people and listening to their questions and objections, you will learn more about how to sell your product in that first 100 calls than someone else might learn in one or two years.

You Will Start to Sell

The second wonderful thing that will happen is that, because you are making no effort to sell, you will start to make sales almost without effort. Your confidence and energy will increase with each call you make. Your self-esteem will be augmented. You will feel more calm and comfortable. As a result, you will like your customers, and they will like you and want to buy from you. By the time you have made 100 calls, you will have turbocharged your sales career and be on your way to the top.

Here is something else I have found. For the next two years, you will find yourself making sales to many of those on whom you called during your 100-call warm-up period. Because you were relaxed and put them under no pressure to buy, they relaxed as well, and they thought of you when they decided to buy what you were selling.

Break Out of a Slump

You can use this 100-call method to break out of a sales slump, or to start off a new sales year or even a new sales period. At any time, you can turbocharge yourself by setting a goal to make 100 face-to-face calls as fast as you possibly can without worrying about whether or not you make a sale. There is something about this strategy that releases your potential and enables you to perform at your best.

When you combine the 100-call method with all of the other psychological techniques that we have talked about in this book so far, you will become a remarkable salesperson. You will have vigor, zeal, confidence, and competence at a level that you may never have experienced before. You will have taken complete charge of your sales career and put yourself in field position to earn more than you ever have.

Action Exercises:

1. Resolve today that you are going to become one of the hardest-working professional salespeople in your industry; start earlier; work harder; stay later.

2. Make a plan today to go out and call on 100 new prospects as fast as you can; make it a game to see more people in the next month than anyone else in your business.

3. Accept 100 percent responsibility for your work and your life, and refuse to make excuses for any reason; see yourself as the president of your own personal sales corporation.

4. Start your own personal development library of books and audios, and devote yourself to lifelong learning.

5. Make sure that you are selling the right product for you, tangible or intangible; does it excite and motivate you to sell it each day?

6. Think and act long term in your sales work, and in your life; imagine that you are going to be selling to the same people for the next twenty years.

7. Develop unshakable persistence; resolve in advance that you will never give up until you are a big success in your sales career.

....

There is no failure except in no longer trying. There is no defeat except from within, no really insurmountable barrier except for our own inherent weakness of purpose.

—Elbert Hubbard

....

2

THE PSYCHOLOGY OF CLOSING

We learn wisdom from failure much more than from success. We often discover what will work, by finding out what will not work; and probably he who never made a mistake never made a discovery.

—Samuel Smiles

CLOSING IS OFTEN THE MOST PAINFUL PART OF THE sales presentation. It is the part that most salespeople dislike the most. They become reluctant to proceed. They freeze up and lose their feeling of control over the buying process.

The prospect also dislikes having to make a buying decision. As you get closer and closer to the end of the sales presentation, he becomes nervous as well. Your job as a sales professional is to structure the presentation in such a way that you move smoothly through the close and wrap up the sale.

Closing is very much like a bump at the end of the road of the sales conversation. You have established rapport, identified needs, presented your product, and answered objections. Now you have to wrap up the transaction and get the order. As you approach this final bump, your task is to take the prospect past this point as quickly as possible.

Don't Draw It Out

There is a story of an old gentleman who calls up his long-time dentist and says, "Bill, I've got this rotten tooth, and it's got to come out. I just wondered how much you charge nowadays to pull a tooth?"

His dentist friend replies, "Well, Jack, it's eighty dollars to pull a tooth."

Jack says, "Wow! That's a lot of money. How long does it take?"

"It takes about one minute."

"Eighty dollars for one minute?" Jack cries. "That's an awful lot of money for that small amount of time."

"Well, Jack," says the dentist, "if it's the amount of time that concerns you, I can take *all the time* you'd like."

MAKE IT SMOOTH AND PAINLESS

You have an obligation to your customers to move smoothly through the close and to assure that it is as quick and painless as possible. To minimize stress for both of you, you must make it fast and efficient. This is a key part of your job.

There is always a period of tension at the end of the sales process. For you as a salesperson, the close represents the culmination of all your efforts. The idea of losing the sale can be very stressful. You start to feel tense. Your stomach churns. Your solar plexus tightens up. Sometimes your heart rate increases, and your throat goes dry. Because you are asking the customer to take action, and he may say no, the whole idea of closing triggers a tremendous fear of failure.

You have an obligation to your customers to move smoothly through the close and to assure that it is as quick and painless as possible.

The shorter the closing process, the less stress you experience. Take the prospect through the close promptly. Fortunately, this is a selling skill that you can learn with input and practice.

Once you have explained your product, and the prospect's buying desire has been aroused, move briskly *past* the close and into wrapping up the details of the purchase.

REVERSE ENGINEER YOUR PRESENTATION

The key is to plan your close in advance. And instead of planning your sales presentation first and *then* your close, plan your close and *then* your sales presentation. Decide how you are going to ask for the order, and then "reverse engineer" your sales presentation. Start with the end in mind. Then go back to the beginning and organize your sales presentation so that it arrives logically at your closing question.

Take the time to think through exactly how you are going to ask for the order when it is clear that the prospect is fully informed and ready to buy. Plan and rehearse your closing technique(s) so that you can do it in your sleep. Top sales professionals have their closes planned word for word, in advance. So should you.

Amateur salespeople, those who spin their wheels in frustration year after year, tend to fly by the seat of their pants in every sales conversation. When it comes time to ask for the order, their hearts pound, their foreheads sweat, and they say whatever comes out of their mouths. They then cross their fingers, hoping and praying that the prospect will buy. Professional salespeople proceed through the presentation, and through the close, in a single smooth, well-prepared process.

Six Major Requirements for Closing

1. You must be positive, enthusiastic, and eager to close the sale. Emotions are contagious. When it is clear that you intensely desire to make this sale, your desire will have a positive effect on the behavior of your prospect.

2. The prospect's requirements must be clear to you. As a result of asking and listening, you should know

exactly what this prospect wants and needs from
your product.

3. The prospect must understand your offer and the
   value of your product or service to her. She must be
   absolutely clear about what your product does to
   change and improve her life or work.

4. The prospect must believe and trust you. There
   must be a high degree of rapport and friendship.
   In addition, the prospect must have faith in your
   company and believe that they will deliver on
   your promises.

5. The prospect must desire to enjoy the advantages
   and benefits of your offer. He must want what you
   are selling. There is no point in trying to close a sale
   if the prospect is not intensely interested in benefiting from your product or service.

6. The product must be suited to the customer, ideal
   for her needs, capacity to pay, and circumstances. It
   must be clear to the prospect that this product or
   service is the right choice for her at this time.

Only when you have fulfilled these six requirements can
you move confidently into closing the sale. If any of them
has not been achieved, the prospect will refuse to buy.

Closing Too Early

Think of visiting a typical used car lot. You stop to look at a car for just a moment, and suddenly a salesperson emerges and says, "That's a good choice; why don't you buy it?"

After you ask the closing question, you must then be completely quiet. Don't say a word. Allow the silence to build up if necessary, because whoever speaks first, loses.

In a situation like this, you don't know anything about the car, and the salesperson doesn't know anything about you. He is asking you to make an offer or buy the car before you know anything about it.

Attempting to close before you are fully aware of what you are buying does not arouse buying desire. Quite the opposite; you feel insulted, and your first impulse is to simply walk away.

Avoid High Pressure

There are four things you must be sure of before you ask a closing question:

First, the prospect must *want* it.

Second, the prospect must *need* it.

Third, the prospect must be able to *afford* it.

And fourth, the prospect must be able to *use it* and get full value out of your product or service.

If you ask for the order before these four requirements have been determined, you will often kill the sale.

Use Silence After a Closing Question

The only pressure that you are allowed to use as a sales professional is the pressure of the silence that takes place after the closing question.

After you ask the closing question, you must then be completely quiet. Don't say a word. Allow the silence to build up if necessary, because whoever speaks first, loses.

Once upon a time, the president of a fast-growing company was considering the purchase of a $750,000 computer system to automate every aspect of his national business. The company that was bidding for the job had done everything exactly right. The salesperson had established rapport, identified the customer's needs, done a full analysis, checked it out in every detail, and prepared a complete proposal for the customer to consider. They had arranged the final appointment, and the salesperson was coming in to close the sale.

The president of the prospect company had started his career in sales when he was younger. He was curious to see how this computer salesman was going to close a $750,000 sale. In the final presentation and discussion, the president had his controller and his accountant present to go over the final details. The salesman came in with his engineer and computer programmer. They sat down and began.

As the salesman went through the proposal, he explained how it would be installed, what would be involved, the warranties and guarantees, the help and service they would provide, the additional consulting that was available, and every other detail of the purchase. He gave him the price and explained what it included. Finally he said, "If you like what I have shown you, then if you'll just authorize this contract, we'll get started on it right away."

He then put a tick mark next to the signature line, put his pen on the contract, and pushed it across the desk to the president.

The Silent Close

The president could see it coming. He thought to himself, *He is going to use the silent close on me.* He knew exactly what the salesperson was doing, so he just looked at him and smiled.

The salesman and the president sat there silently, smiling at each other, for what seemed like an eternity. The silence lasted fifteen minutes. Neither one of them said a word. Neither of the other people present said a word either. They had all been prepared.

Finally, the president smiled, picked up the pen, and signed the contract. At that point, they both laughed. So did everyone else. The tension was broken, and the deal was done.

The pressure of the silence after the closing question is often the most powerful sales tool you have for concluding the transaction. But you must be disciplined. Once you ask a closing question, you must not "step on your lines" by adding anything. Just wait quietly for the prospect to respond.

Recognizing Buying Signals

There are several common buying signals that the prospect will give off to let you know that he is on the verge of making a decision. Relax and be aware of these signals when they come. They tell you that it is time to ask a closing question.

RAPID TALKING

The prospect will often start talking faster. He may brighten up and become more positive and cheerful. In his mind, he has reached a decision, and the inner tension has been broken. Whenever a customer shifts from thoughtful or critical to positive and happy, you can speak up and ask a closing question.

SUDDEN FRIENDLINESS

The customer engages in "sudden friendliness." She seems to relax, shift gears, and may ask you a personal or friendly question. "How long have you been in town?" "Do you have kids in school?" "Would you like another cup of coffee?"

Whenever you experience this sudden friendliness, you should respond warmly and positively, and then ask a closing question. "Thank you. I will have another cup of coffee. And by the way, how soon would you need this?"

CHIN RUBBING

Chin rubbing is another sign that the customer is approaching a buying decision. Whenever a prospect goes into deep thought, his hand comes to his chin and his head goes down. If you are talking with a prospect and he begins rubbing his chin and thinking, stop talking immediately. Your customer has now gone *inward* and is no longer listening to you. If you continue to speak, you will sound like a droning noise in the room, like a big bee trying to get out the window. Instead, become perfectly silent.

> *If you are talking with a prospect and he begins rubbing his chin and thinking, stop talking immediately. Your customer has now gone* inward *and is no longer listening to you.*

While the customer is rubbing his chin, he is processing your offer. He is thinking through how he can buy your product, how he can pay for it, how he will use it, where he will put it, and so on. When his hand comes down from his chin, his head comes up, and you make eye contact with him, in 99 percent of cases, the decision to buy has been made.

At this point, smile and ask a closing question, such as, "How soon do you need this?" Then sit silently until you get confirmation.

QUESTIONS ABOUT PRICE, TERMS, OR DELIVERY

The most common buying signals are when the prospect asks you about *price, terms,* or *delivery.*

"How much does this cost, exactly?

"What sort of terms can I get on this purchase?"

"How long does it take to get one of these if I decide to buy it?"

Whenever the prospect asks you a question involving price, terms, or delivery, turn it into a closing question by asking about one of the three subjects that the client did not mention.

For example, the prospect asks, "How much does this cost?"

You reply, "How soon do you need it?"

When the prospect says, "By the end of the month," the sale is made.

Remember that *the person who asks questions has control.* Here is the key. Always try to answer a question with a question. This enables you to get more information and often close the sale. But most importantly, it allows you to keep control of the sales conversation.

Prospect: "How soon can I get this?"

You: "How many did you want?"

If the prospect gives you a specific number, you've just made a sale.

CHANGE IN ATTITUDE, POSTURE, OR VOICE

Any noticeable change in *attitude, posture,* or *voice* can indicate that a buying decision is near. If the prospect sits up straight or begins calculating numbers, you can test to be sure that this is a buying signal by asking,

"By the way, how soon do you need this?"

"Would you want us to get started on this right away?"

"How many of these would you like?"

"Would you prefer that we deliver this to your office or to your warehouse?"

Whenever you see a prospect changing his *demeanor* or *body language* in any way, moving in his chair, brightening up, or becoming friendly, assume that the decision has been made and ask a question to confirm it.

Why the Close Is Difficult

There are several reasons why the close is the most difficult and stressful part of the sale. The first of these is the salesperson's natural *fear of rejection*. We are conditioned from childhood to be highly sensitive to the ways we are treated by others, especially to their approval or disapproval.

This begins with our parents and then transfers to our bosses and our customers. As adults, at an unconscious level, we are very concerned about being liked and accepted by others. The possibility of rejection is something that causes us tremendous stress, and that we make every effort to avoid.

REJECTION IS NOT PERSONAL

When I was just starting out in sales, and extremely nervous, an experienced salesperson told me something that changed my course. He said, "Remember, no matter what a prospect says, *rejection is not personal.*"

Wow! That was an important point. "Rejection is not personal."

A prospect cannot reject you *as a person* because the prospect does not even know who you are or what you are selling. All the prospect is doing is responding to a commercial offer in a competitive society where he is overwhelmed with people trying to sell him things. When he says something like, "I'm not interested," it doesn't mean anything; it is not a reflection on your ability or character. It is just a natural, knee-jerk reaction to any sales offering.

Fully one-third of salespeople drop out of selling each year because they cannot deal with the rejection that is part and parcel of the business. Top salespeople, however, continually remind themselves that rejection is not personal, and they don't let it bother them.

FAILURE IS ONLY FEEDBACK

The second reason closing is hard is because of the *fear of failure*, of trying and not succeeding. It is the fear of losing your time, your effort, and even your money, of making an investment of energy and emotion in a prospect and losing it completely when the prospect decides not to buy from you.

The fear of failure, coupled with the fear of rejection, is the primary reason people underachieve or fail in life. It is only when you get over these two fears that you begin to realize your full potential in sales, and in every other area.

Keep reminding yourself that there is no such thing as failure; there is only *feedback*. When you try something that doesn't work, look into the experience for the valuable lesson you can learn, and then let it go. Say to yourself, *Some will. Some won't. So what? Next!*

Overcome Your Fears

Ralph Waldo Emerson once wrote, "Do the thing you fear and the death of fear is certain." This is one of the most important success principles ever discovered. The only way that you can eliminate a fear that might be holding you back is to do the thing that you fear. The death of fear is *certain*.

Both courage and cowardice are *habits*. You can develop the habit of courage by confronting your fears and moving toward them rather than hiding from your fears and moving away from them, as most people do. As Mark Twain once said, "Courage is not absence of fear; it is control of fear, mastery of fear."

DO THE THING YOU FEAR

Make more calls, and you will experience less fear of making calls. If you keep making calls, as many as possible, day after day, without really caring whether the prospect responds in a positive or negative way, you eventually reach the point at which you have no fear at all. By confronting your fears of failure and rejection, you eventually develop habitual courage. At this point, you will turn a corner in your career, and your sales will begin to go up rapidly.

Once you have developed courage as a habit, along with the ability to face your fears of failure and rejection, your whole life will improve. You will feel terrific about yourself. Your self-esteem and self-confidence will swell. And as you improve on the inside, your sales results will improve on the outside.

Why Customers Don't Buy

The fear of failure is also a major reason why people don't buy. They are afraid of making a mistake, of purchasing the wrong article. They are fearful of paying too much or of being criticized for making the wrong choice.

Every prospect has made buying mistakes in the past. She has bought things that she wishes she hadn't. She has been left in the lurch after a purchase, unable to get support or service, and sorry that she ever dealt with that company in the first place.

YOU MUST OVERCOME CUSTOMER FEARS

When you go to see a new prospect, you have to deal with the fact that this prospect has had all these difficult and challenging past sales experiences. You must not only arouse buying desire for your product, but you must overcome all the fears this prospect has, based on his previous experience, of making a mistake.

How many times have you heard a prospect say, "I have to talk it over with someone else before I make a decision"?

Husbands will not buy a product until they have talked to their wives. Wives will not buy a product until they are sure their husbands will approve. Managers will not OK a purchase until their bosses have agreed to it. Many people cannot make a buying decision at all until they have gotten the approval and assurance from everyone around them. This is how customers deal with the twin fears of failure and rejection.

Customers Become Comfortable

Another major obstacle to closing is *human inertia*. If a person is comfortable using a particular product or service, it is much easier for him to continue with what he is doing than to make a change. People get into a comfort zone. They become accustomed to their current methods. You may have a cheaper or better product, but the advantages and benefits you offer are often not enough to get the prospect to change his existing way of doing things.

To get a prospect to change from one product or service to another, from one way of doing things to a different way, you must emphasize all the additional benefits that he will enjoy. The attractiveness of the benefits must be so great that they motivate the prospect enough to do something different. You may have to return several times, continually repeating and emphasizing the benefits and advantages of your offer to get the prospect to finally make the transition.

Buying Can Be Stressful

Another common obstacle to closing is the stress involved in making a buying decision. Since the buying decision involves an irrevocable commitment of assets, and limits the freedom and flexibility of the prospect, people always become a bit nervous when it comes to making the final decision. When people feel the stress of making an important commitment, they often tense up and push it away, saying, "Leave it with me; let me think about it."

Because of these psychological obstacles to closing, both on your part and on the part of the prospect, you must be positive, confident, and professional at every stage of the sales process. You must especially move quickly through the close to wrapping up the details rather than leaving the closing decision hanging in the air. In everything you do, make it easy for the customer to say yes.

The Prospect Is Always Right

Never tell the prospect that he is *wrong*. Never argue with him. And never look at selling as a competition that you need to win. No matter what the prospect says about your product or service, remain relaxed and cheerful. Don't tell him that his assessment of your product is incorrect. Instead say, "That's a very valid concern, Mr. Prospect. Many of our customers have had the same concern, and here is how we have taken care of it."

There is an old saying: "A man convinced against his will, is of the same opinion still." If you argue and overwhelm the customer with your brilliant response, the prospect may nod and agree with you, but she will still end up not buying.

Instead of debating a point with regard to price or quality with your prospect, find a way to neutralize the concern. Answer the objection to her satisfaction. Show her that she need not worry about the part of your offering that she is challenging.

USE TESTIMONIAL LETTERS

Perhaps the most powerful tool you can use to overcome objections and concerns is testimonial letters from satisfied clients who had the same concern when you first spoke to them. Sometimes we call these *sweetheart letters*. If you have made a sale and you have a good relationship with the customer, go back and ask him if he would write a sweetheart letter for you. You can even offer to write the letter yourself and have the customer put it on his own letterhead.

Never tell the prospect that he is wrong. Never argue with him. And never look at selling as a competition that you need to win.

In the sweetheart letter, you take a common objection that you get, such as high price, and have a customer give you a letter that says something like this:

Dear Brian,

When I first spoke to you about your product, I was concerned about your high price in comparison with other products available in the market. But I decided to go ahead anyway, and I am certainly glad I did. We have found that your higher price is

more than justified by all the additional features and benefits that
we have experienced with your product since we started using it.
Sincerely,
A Happy Customer

Show this to your prospect when the question of high price comes up. It will often demolish her concerns.

TESTIMONIALS ARE PROOF

As a general rule, the prospect will discount anything you say about your product or service. After all, you are a salesperson. You are expected to speak positively about what you are selling.

But if someone *else* says something good about your product, especially in writing, that is considered to be a valid statement. Third-party proof, in the form of testimonial letters, is a powerful way to convince people of the goodness and value of what you are selling. This is why it is said that "salespeople who don't use testimonial letters have skinny kids."

Keep Your Opinions to Yourself

A common error to avoid is expressing your opinions to a prospect on subjects of a personal nature. The basic rule is to avoid the subjects of *religion, politics,* or *sex.* Even if you feel strongly about one of these areas, and your prospect wants to talk about the subject, make every effort to remain neutral. You can nod and agree with the prospect's opinion, but don't feed the fire by adding comments of your own. Instead, gently bring the conversation back around to your product or service by asking questions that relate to this area. Keep your opinions to yourself.

Always Be Complimentary

Never knock your competition. In fact, you should do the opposite. If your competitor's name is brought up in the conversation, and the prospect asks, "What do you think about ABC Company?" always reply positively. You could say, "Mr. Prospect, ABC is an excellent company. They have good products, and they have been around for a long time. However, we believe that our product is superior to ABC's in three specific ways. Let me show them to you." You then concentrate on selling the values and benefits of your product or service, but without saying anything negative about your competitor's. When you speak positively about your competitors, customers view you in a more positive way than someone who criticizes their competitors.

Don't Assume Authority

The final closing error to avoid is assuming authority that you don't have. It is making promises that you can't keep. It is overselling your product, saying that your product can do something that it cannot do.

Not long ago, an office equipment saleswoman lost a $10,000 sale with my company because of overpromising. In the course of discussing the specifications for the machine, my office manager asked her if it could do two-sided copying. She assured her that it could. But when we looked at the specifications more closely, we found that it definitely did *not* do double-sided copying. The saleswoman had not taken the time to fully understand what she was selling. Not only did she lose the sale, but she lost an enormous amount of credibility. Don't let this happen to you.

More Obstacles to Closing

Another major obstacle to closing is *negative expectations*. These occur when the salesperson decides in advance that this particular prospect is not going to buy. He prejudges the prospect based on his initial attitude or his physical surroundings. Perhaps the prospect is not stylish or well-groomed. Maybe the office or its furniture is old or cluttered. The salesperson leaps to the conclusion that this is not a good prospect and stops making any real effort to conclude the sale.

Remember the law of expectations, which says, "Whatever you expect, with confidence, becomes your own self-fulfilling prophecy."

Your expectations exert an undue influence on the people around you. The expectations of other people, especially people whom you look up to and respect, have an extraordinary influence on you as well. Your expectations determine your attitude, and your attitude determines how you treat other people.

EXPECT THE BEST

The rule with regard to expectations is to always *expect the best!* Expect that people will like you. Look forward to people being attracted to your product or service. Anticipate people asking you tough questions prior to buying. Then expect to be successful more often than not. Incorporate an attitude of *positive expectancy* into your sales activities, and people will treat you better . . . as you expected. You'll also make more sales.

But when you make the mistake of negatively prejudging a prospect, you lose your enthusiasm. Your attitude comes across as that of someone who doesn't really believe in the sale or the prospect's ability to buy what you are selling. The prospect picks up this attitude from you and fulfills your prophecy. He declines to buy.

Great Results from Small Beginnings

A friend of mine sells personnel placement services. He called on an industrial building in a warehouse area one day only to find that the warehouse was fairly unoccupied. There was only one man, seated behind a desk in a small office off the main entrance. There were no other offices and no partitions. The building was empty.

Since my friend was already there, he confidently knocked on the door and introduced himself to the one man who was there. They began talking about his business. He told the prospect that he was in the business of personnel selection. Their specialty was to find and place both technical and nontechnical personnel for industrial corporations. They had the ability to staff a company with engineers, technical employees, and draftspersons, as well as with secretaries, accountants, and bookkeepers. They focused on manufacturing and construction companies.

DON'T PREJUDGE THE PROSPECT

The lone prospect said, "Well, we have nothing going on right now. I have just been sent out here from the East to open this office. We are working on a major contract, and we have high hopes, but we don't have anything firmed up as of yet.

"If you would like to call back in the next couple of weeks, I will be here. Please keep in touch; we may have need of your services sometime in the future."

My friend approached everything with an attitude of positive expectancy. He called back every couple of weeks, and when he was in that area, he would often drop in and have a cup of coffee. Each time he'd get the same answer. The company was still waiting to finalize a couple of large contracts.

Nonetheless, he always treated the prospect well. He brought him information and gave him prices on his services. He called him on a regular basis and kept in touch with him by phone.

One day he walked in and the prospect said, "I am so glad you are here! We just got a $50 million contract for design, engineering, and construction, and we're going to have to hire seventy workers over the next sixty days. Can you help us?"

He was ready. He made more than $200,000 in commissions over the next sixty days hiring and placing technical staff for this company. He earned more from that one contract than he was accustomed to making for two years of hard work. Keeping a positive attitude toward prospective customers is good business.

Keep Your Chin Up

Lack of enthusiasm is yet another major barrier to closing. Nothing will kill a sale faster than a salesperson who doesn't seem to care about making the sale in the first place. Often this lack of enthusiasm is the result of *fatigue*.

To succeed in selling, you must have energy. You must really *want* to close sales. You must really crave the business. You must feel strongly that what you are selling is really advantageous for your customer. You must be keen and eager and possess the kind of emotional commitment that makes it clear to the prospect that you want to do business with him.

Never forget, selling is hard work. It is extraordinarily draining. Several hours of interacting with customers can tire you out completely. At the end of the day, you can be quite exhausted.

For this reason, if you are going to *sell* five days a week, you should *go to bed* early five days a week. Turn off the television, shut down the house, and get to bed by 10:00 PM. Get eight full hours of sleep prior to every selling day. When you are fully rested, you will have far more energy than at any other time. You will be ready to perform at your best.

The Customer Comes First

The ability to close a sale can also be hindered by a *lack of sincerity*. This often occurs when the salesperson becomes more concerned about earning the commission than with benefiting the customer. As soon as a salesperson begins to see the prospect as a source of money rather than as a person who needs help with a product or service, her tone of voice, body language, and attitude change. Once the salesperson starts thinking about the commission, the prospect starts feeling like a fish in a bowl with a cat looking on.

> *If you are going to* sell *five days a week, you should* go to bed *early five days a week. Turn off the television, shut down the house, and get to bed by* 10:00 PM. *Get eight full hours of sleep prior to every selling day.*

Prospects are very perceptive. They pick up emotional vibrations from the salesperson. Prospects know when you are trying to help *them*, as opposed to trying to make a sale that will help *you*. It is essential that you keep your mind focused on what you can do for your customer. The sale and the commission will follow naturally.

Different Wavelengths

A common hindrance to closing arises when you find yourself with a prospect that is on a different wavelength from you. One of the most important rules I ever learned in sales was that "many people are prospects, but they are not all *your* prospects."

Sometimes there is positive chemistry between you and the prospect; sometimes there is not. This does not mean that there is anything wrong with either of you. There is simply a *mismatch* of temperament. Somehow the two of you don't get along very well. No matter how pleasant and polite you are, you find it impossible to build a friendly relationship.

> *Many people are prospects, but they are not all your prospects.*

Perhaps you are well educated, but you are talking to an uneducated prospect. You may be an analytical person who finds yourself speaking with a people-driven or results-oriented individual. Maybe you are brisk, but your prospect is laid-back. This happens more often than not.

SAVE THE PROSPECT FOR YOUR COMPANY

If you find yourself on a different wavelength from your prospect, don't take it personally. It will happen a lot. When it does happen, if you feel that the prospect is a good candidate for what you sell, try to save her for your company.

Instead of trying to build a relationship where it is not possible, suggest someone else in your company who is the "real expert" in this area. Who could get along better with this prospect? Introduce them to each other. You will be amazed at how many sales you can save by handing off a good prospect to someone else with whom she may have better chemistry.

Practice Tag-Team Selling

Many companies practice what is called *tag-team selling*. No prospect is allowed to permanently depart without having spoken to at least *two* salespeople. As soon as a salesperson realizes that he is not hitting it off with a particular customer, he quickly withdraws and suggests that the customer talk with someone else, whom he introduces as "someone who knows a lot more about this product than I do."

Tag-team selling is used when there seems to be a difference or conflict of personalities. Sometimes the customer doesn't like the salesperson, and the salesperson recognizes this. Maybe the salesperson doesn't like the customer, which makes it impossible to sell. Occasionally, an older customer will not like a younger salesperson, or a woman will prefer to be sold to by another woman. Be alert and sensitive to the possibility that you and the customer are not right for each other, and try to save the sale for your company.

LIKING IS ESSENTIAL

There is an important truth in selling: *you can never sell to someone you don't like.* If you don't genuinely like and care about the prospect and sincerely want to help that prospect improve his or her life or work, you will not be successful selling to that person. No matter how hard you try or how warmly you smile, something about your attitude will give off negative vibrations that the prospect will pick up.

Whenever you find that there is lack of chemistry between you and a prospect, accept it as an unavoidable fact of life. If you are in a retail environment, excuse yourself for a moment and come back with someone else the prospect may like better than you. If you are calling on a prospect and you feel a lack of rapport, ask the prospect if you could come back and bring someone "who knows more than I do."

In every case, get your ego out of the way. Focus on helping the customer solve his problem or satisfy his need by finding the right person to work with him. This is the mark of the true professional.

Once you have taken full control of your thinking and resolved to make sure that the prospect is ready to buy, you can proceed to the last big obstacle, answering objections.

Action Exercises:

1. Analyze your previous customers; what do your best customers have in common, and how could you spend more time with more people like them?

2. Identify your major competitors and determine at least three advantages that your products have over theirs; make these clear when your prospect mentions one of them.

3. Overcome your fear of rejection by confronting the fear over and over again; the more you do this, the more you realize that rejection is not personal.

4. Eliminate your fears of failure by developing the habit of doing whatever you are afraid to do; act as if it were impossible to fail, and it shall be.

5. Expect the best in every sales situation; treat every prospect as if he has the ability to buy a million dollars' worth of what you sell.

6. Ask for testimonial letters from your satisfied customers; carry them with you and show them to neutralize sales resistance.

7. Identify the major fears that your prospects have that hold them back from buying, and then find a way to neutralize those fears.

It is better to conquer yourself than to win a thousand battles. Then the victory is yours. It cannot be taken from you, not by angels or by demons, heaven or hell.
—Gautama Buddha

3

HOW TO HANDLE ANY OBJECTION

Victory becomes, to some degree, a state of mind.
Know ourselves superior to the anxieties, troubles and
worries which obsess us, we are superior to them.

—Basil King

THERE ARE NO SALES WITHOUT OBJECTIONS. OBJECTIONS indicate interest. Objections are signposts that lead you step-by-step toward closing the sale. The fact is, if there are no objections, there is no interest. If there is no interest, there will be no sale.

In reality, successful sales have twice as many objections as unsuccessful sales. The more objections you get, the more likely it is that you are moving toward actually making the sale.

The Law of Six

There is a Law of Six that applies to objections. This law says that there are never more than six objections to any offering. There may be one or two, but there are never more than six.

Even if you hear fifty or one hundred objections in the course of a week or a month, all of these objections can be clustered into a small number of categories.

In working with companies, we sometimes engage in a sentence completion exercise. We ask them to complete this sentence: "We could sell to every qualified prospect we talked to as long as they just didn't say . . ."

Make a list of every single objection that a qualified prospect could give you to avoid making a buying decision. Write down every question, criticism, or complaint you have heard. Once you have this list, organize it by priority. What are the most common objections? Which ones stand most in the way of your making a sale?

CLUSTER THE OBJECTIONS

Once you have prioritized them, cluster the objections into categories. You may have price objections, quality objections, competitive objections, capability objections, reputation objections, or newness objections. Determine the clusters for your objections and then sort out your objections into each of these clusters. It will never be more than six separate clusters.

Your job now is to develop a *bulletproof answer* for each of your major objections. Determine exactly what your prospect must be convinced of for this objection to be removed as an obstacle to proceeding with the purchase. Whatever you need to do to eliminate your major objections, begin doing it immediately.

Use a Testimonial

As you already know, one of the most powerful ways to eliminate objections is to present testimonial letters from satisfied customers who shared that objection at one time. A sweetheart letter answering a customer's major concern is a potent way to demolish the objection forever.

Interpret It as a Question

Aside from using testimonials, another way to deal with objections is for you to take the objection and interpret it as a question. Treat it as a request for more information. Recognize that an objection is a natural customer response to any offering where there is some risk of purchasing.

When the prospect says, "It costs too much," you can respond by saying, "That's a good question. Why does it seem to cost more than you expected to pay?" You then go on to answer the question that you have posed.

If the prospect says, "We can get it cheaper elsewhere," you say, "That's a good question. Why does it appear that our competitors sell a similar product for less?"

GIVE A GOOD REASON

Another way to deal with an objection is to treat it as if the customer is asking you for a reason to eliminate the objection. If the customer says, "I can't afford it," you can imagine that the customer is really saying, "Show me how I can justify spending this amount of money."

When a customer says, "I have to talk it over with someone else," imagine that what the prospect means is, "Please give me sufficient reason to buy this so that I don't have to check and get someone else's opinion."

MAKE IT EASY TO OBJECT

Above all, make it easy to object. Most customers do not want to get into an argument or a debate with you over your product or service. They will be reluctant to object for fear that you will become upset or adamant. For this reason you must make it easy for the customer to object by responding in a cheerful, friendly, constructive way when he does.

Objections are not to be feared. Rather, they are the stepping-stones on the road to sales success, the rungs on the ladder to high earnings. The very best salespeople are those who have learned to deal with objections in the fastest and most effective way.

COMPLIMENT THE OBJECTION

Compliment each objection when you hear it for the first time. "That's a good point; I'm glad you mentioned that." As

Abraham Lincoln said, "Everybody likes a compliment." When you compliment people for bringing up objections or questions about your product or service, you make them feel better about themselves. As a result, they feel more comfortable asking you additional questions. But just like a trial lawyer, who never asks a question he doesn't already know

> When you compliment people for bringing up objections or questions about your product or service, you make them feel better about themselves.

the answer to, never go into a sales situation without knowing how to answer the main objections you are going to hear.

LISTEN CAREFULLY

When you get an objection, hear it out *completely*. Don't assume that you know what the prospect is going to say. Often the prospect will begin with an objection you've heard before, but then will add her own particular concern or problem at the end. Be patient. Practice your listening skills. Pause before replying. Question for clarification: "How do you mean?" Feed it back in your own words to prove to the prospect that you were listening and that you understand her real concern.

OBJECTION VERSUS CONDITION

Determine whether the customer's response is an objection or a *condition*. An objection is something that you can answer. It is a problem for which there is a solution. It is an obstacle that can be removed on the way to making the sale.

A condition, however, is a genuine reason for not going ahead. If a company is going into bankruptcy, it cannot buy your product or service. No matter how good it is, bankruptcy creates a condition that makes it impossible to proceed. If a person has no money, this is a condition that renders buying not possible.

But here's an interesting discovery: when a prospect voices an objection, he often only *thinks* it is a genuine condition. He believes that because of this obstacle, he cannot buy what you are selling. This is seldom true.

For example, when a prospect says, "I can't afford it" what does this mean? Does it mean that he can't afford it at this moment, or that he cannot afford the full price in one payment? That he cannot afford it today, but he can afford it sometime in the future? When a person says, "I can't afford it," always respond with "How do you mean, exactly?"

MY MILLION-DOLLAR POLICY

One day an insurance salesman was introduced to me by a mutual friend. He asked me a series of questions and then arranged a follow-up appointment. At this second meeting, he presented me with a proposal for one million dollars in life insurance. I almost fell off my chair!

I told him, "This is far too much. I can't afford it."

Ignoring my initial sales resistance, he explained to me that I would be unwise in my position, with a wife and two children, to have less than one million dollars' worth of insurance. I finally agreed that I needed that amount, but I repeated, "I can't afford it. I don't have the three thousand dollars' premium available. Thank you, but it's not possible at this time."

He said, "What if we structured it on a monthly basis and I could get it for you for $250 per month? Would that work out all right for you?" Quite honestly, I was surprised. At that time I had only heard of life insurance costs based on *annual* premiums. I had no idea that I could pay for it on a monthly basis. What I thought was a genuine condition, a reason for not buying, turned out to be merely an objection for which there was a logical and workable answer. I signed the application form and purchased the insurance immediately.

Use Your Creativity

Here is the point. Because your prospects are not aware of all the different ways they can acquire and pay for your product or service, they are often convinced that they "can't afford it." It is only when you show them that there are options available that they will turn around and buy what you are selling.

For example, the prospect says, "I can't afford the monthly payments." You say, "What if we could spread the payments over three years instead of two, and get them below five hundred dollars a month? Would you be able to handle that?"

When you get an objection, and you've heard it out

completely, ask the prospect to elaborate in greater detail. This is where "How do you mean?" is very helpful. Be sure you fully understand the thinking behind the objection before you attempt to answer it. If you answer too soon, you may be answering the wrong concern and actually driving the sale away.

BE POLITE AND RESPECTFUL

Treat every objection with kindness, courtesy, and respect. Be low-keyed and sensitive. Even if you have heard the objection a thousand times, always respond as though it is a valuable and worthwhile comment on your offering.

You have heard the old saying "People don't care how much you know until they know how much you care." When you handle their objections with warmth and tact, prospects realize that you genuinely care about how they feel. As a result, they will begin to genuinely care about you and the product or service you represent.

THE FEEL, FELT, FOUND METHOD

An excellent way of dealing with objections is to use the "feel, felt, found" method. This is a professional way of acknowledging the objection as being valid, assuring the prospect that she is not alone in her concern, and then answering the objection in a satisfactory way.

For example, the prospect could say, "It costs too much." You respond by saying, "Mrs. Prospect, I understand exactly how you *feel*. Others *felt* the same way when we first spoke to them. But this is what they *found*." Then go on to explain that people with the same concern discovered that even though they paid a little more than they had expected to, they were very happy with their decision because they got so much more in value.

Prospects are inordinately influenced by what other people have done with regard to your product or service. When you assure them that others have felt the same way, gone ahead and purchased your product, and were happy with the results, they relax and begin believing that this product would be good for them as well.

Use It with Many Objections

What if a prospect says, "Everybody offers great service, but then they don't follow up; I have been left in the lurch too many times"?

"Mr. Prospect, I understand exactly how you *feel*. Others *felt* the same way about our follow-up service. It is a major consideration in making a purchase like this. But what our customers have *found* is that we service and repair this item within two hours, up to three o'clock in the afternoon during any business day. And if it is after three, we will have someone there first thing in the morning."

Whenever possible, provide *proof* for your answer in the form of a testimonial letter, a price comparison, or even a magazine or newspaper article attesting to the quality of your product or service.

Be sure to ask, "Does this answer your question?"

Nine Common Objections You Must Answer:

1. UNSPOKEN OBJECTIONS

The first type of objection you will get is an *unspoken* objection. The customer has concerns with your offering but doesn't tell you anything. He or she nods and listens to you, but you get no feedback to tell you where you are or how you are doing.

The solution to unspoken objections is to let the prospect talk more. Ask open-ended questions, lean forward, and listen intently to the answers. The more a prospect has an opportunity to answer your questions, the more likely it is that she will tell you exactly what might be holding her back from buying.

2. EXCUSES, EXCUSES

The second form of objections is *excuses*. These are usually instinctive reactions to any sales approach.

"We're happy with our existing suppliers."

"We are really busy right now and don't have time to think about it. "

"We already have all we need."

"We are really not interested at the moment."

These are just excuses. They are not really serious. The best salespeople nod, smile, agree, and then ask a question to take control of the conversation. The very best way to handle any initial sales resistance, including excuses and impulse responses is with these words: "That's all right.

Most people in your situation felt the same way when I first called on them. But now they have become our best customers, and they recommend us to their friends."

This response immediately shifts the focus of the conversation away from your product and onto other satisfied customers. It almost invariably triggers the response you want: "Oh really? What is it, then?"

3. MALICIOUS OBJECTIONS

Then there are the *malicious* objections. Because you call on many different people, you will occasionally call on individuals who are unhappy or angry about their current situations. Since they cannot shout at their bosses or spouses, they take it out on the friendly salesperson. These people tend to be negative in their demeanor and behavior. They criticize your product or compare it unfavorably to those of your competitors. They sometimes imply that you charge too much or that your product is not of particularly good quality.

The way to deal with malicious objections is to realize that you are not the target. The person you are talking to has problems of his own that have nothing to do with you. You are just caught in the emotional crossfire between him and other factors in his life. Your job, as a professional, is to remain calm, confident, positive, and polite throughout. Very often this behavior on your part will soften the negativity of the prospect and eventually encourage him to open up to you.

4. REQUESTS FOR INFORMATION

The fourth most common objection is a *request for information*. This is the best type of objection for you to hear, because you know how to answer this as well or better than any other part of your presentation.

Whenever a prospect asks for information about the results or benefits she will get from your product or service and how she can get them, you are moving into excellent field position to make a sale.

Use all your objection-handling skills. Welcome the objection. Compliment the person for asking the question. Thank her for bringing it up. And then answer it completely, ending with, "Does that answer your question?"

5. SHOW-OFF OBJECTIONS

Another type of objection is the *show-off* objection. Sometimes prospects try to show you how much they already know about your product or service. They make sophisticated observations or ask you complex questions about your product, service, or industry.

When this happens, respond by taking the *low road*. Show how impressed you are by how much the prospect already knows. Dominate the *listening* and let the prospect dominate the talking. Be conciliatory and polite. Remember, when you make a prospect feel important by listening to him with rapt attention, he is much more likely to warm up and buy from you.

6. Subjective Objections

The sixth most common type of objections are *subjective* or *personal* objections. These objections are aimed at you as a person. Prospects say things such as, "You look like you are doing pretty well in this business." Or "You seem to be making a lot of money selling this product."

Whenever a person becomes critical of you, it could be a sign that you are talking too much about yourself. The prospect is attempting to bring you down a little bit by criticizing your appearance or behavior.

When you find yourself talking too much about your company, your product or service, or your personal life, stop and ask a *question*. Start talking about the customer rather than yourself. Ask questions about what the customer wants and needs. Make the customer the center of attention, and the subjective objections will stop.

7. Objective Objections

You may also hear the *objective* or *factual* objection. These are directed at your product offering and the claims that you make in terms of what it will do for the customer. The prospect may say, "I don't think that it will do the job that we require." Or "It looks good, but it's not satisfactory for our needs."

If you can answer an objective objection, you can often get the sale. The very best way to do this is to provide testimonials and other proof that make it clear that your product *will* do what you say it will. Assure the prospect that she will get the benefits that you promise and you have just made it easier for her to buy from you.

8. GENERAL SALES RESISTANCE

The eighth most common form of objection is what we have called *general sales resistance*. This always occurs at the beginning of a presentation. Until you neutralize this general sales resistance, the customer will be listening to you with a closed mind.

Lower initial sales resistance by using the approach close. Say, "Mr. Prospect, thank you very much for your time. Please relax. I'm not going to try to sell you anything today. All I want to do is ask you some questions and see if there is some way that my company can help you achieve your goals in a cost-effective way. Would that be all right?"

When the prospect relaxes and gives you permission to ask him questions, you immediately begin your preselected open-ended questions to qualify the prospect and find out what he really needs that you can provide for him.

9. LAST-DITCH OBJECTIONS

The final most-common objection is called the *last-ditch* objection. You have made your presentation, and the prospect clearly sees how she would be better off with your product or service. She knows and understands what you are selling and how much you are asking. She is on the verge of making a buying decision, but she still hesitates.

"How do I know I'm getting my money's worth?" she might say. Or "Are you sure this is the best deal I can get?"

Listen with respect; then assure the prospect that yours is an excellent product or service, at a good price, and that everyone else who is using it today is very happy with their decision. You have then overcome the last-ditch objection.

Go Straight to a Closing Question

After you answer an objection, you can often move immediately into a closing question:

"By the way, which of these two did you prefer?"

"Would you prefer that we send the billing to your home or to your office address?"

"Would you like delivery this week, or would next week be better?"

Whatever answer she gives you to one of these questions, the sale is made. You then proceed to completing the paperwork and getting her signature.

Sometimes the last-ditch objection is called a *smoke-screen* objection. Don't overreact. And don't take it too seriously. Smile and say, "Lots of people ask that question when they are buying one of these."

The Remaining-Objections Close

The *remaining-objections close* is quite effective and easy to use. Let us say that you have made your presentation, and the prospect understands your offering and clearly wants to enjoy the benefits that you have presented. But then he says, "I don't know if I should get it now or if I should wait awhile."

To elicit the remaining objections that are holding him back from buying, say, "Mr. Prospect, there seems to be some *question in your mind* that's causing you to hesitate about going ahead right now. Do you mind if I ask what it is—is it the price?" Run these two questions together, asking two questions with just one question mark. The prospect now has to give you an answer and either say, "Yes, it's the price," or "No, it's not that."

Whatever he says, acknowledge his concern and say, "Well, Mr. Prospect, that's an important consideration. And *in addition to that*, is there any other reason that might be causing you to hesitate about going ahead right now?"

SEEK OUT THE REAL REASON

In many cases, the prospect is going to be reluctant to tell you the real reason that he is hesitating. He knows that as soon as he gives it to you and you answer it properly, he will be out of objections and have no choice but to buy what you are offering.

For this reason, a prospect will hold back that remaining objection. He won't want to tell you what it is. He will sometimes give you an unimportant objection, but it is not the real reason that he is hesitating.

No matter how the prospect answers this question, you ask again, "And in addition to *that*, is there any other reason that would cause you to hesitate from going ahead?" You keep asking until he says, "No, that's the last reason." The last reason he gives you in answer to this series of questions is the real or remaining objection: "I'm not sure that we can afford it." Or "I'm not sure that your product will actually do what you say it will."

SATISFY THE FINAL OBJECTION

You then say, "Mr. Prospect, that is an important question. If we could answer that to your complete satisfaction, would you be prepared to go ahead with this?" Remain silent and wait for him to answer.

When the prospect finally says, "Yes, if you can answer that for me, I'm ready to make a buying decision," follow up with this question: "What would it take to satisfy you on that point?" And then again, wait silently for him to give you the "closing condition."

At this stage of the sale, the prospect will almost invariably say, "Well, if you could just do this or that," or "If I could just talk to someone else who has been in the same situation, I'd be ready to go ahead." You now have the closing condition, the key objection, the one factor that you must convince him of to get the sale. You then go ahead and show him that you can answer this objection to his complete satisfaction, and ask for the order.

PRICE OBJECTIONS

Thousands of customers have been interviewed after they have purchased a product or service. During the sales discussion, they asked a lot of questions about the price and terms. But when they were interviewed later and asked, "What was the *real* reason that you decided to buy this product [or service] rather than that of a competitor?" they seldom mentioned price at all.

What we have found is that customers do not want the *lowest* price for a product or service unless it is identical to another product or service. What customers want is a fair price, a good price, the best price, a reasonable price, a competitive price, but not the lowest price. Why is this?

> *What we have found is that customers do not want the lowest price for a product or service unless it is identical to another product or service. What customers want is a fair price, a good price, the best price, a reasonable price, a competitive price, but not the lowest price.*

The reason is because every customer has tried to save money by buying a lower-priced item but ended up getting exactly what he paid for. The product or service was cheap, and the customer was disappointed. The merchandise broke down, or the buyer couldn't get it serviced. In retrospect, he wished he had focused more on higher quality than lower price.

NO ONE WANTS TO OVERPAY

At the same time, no customer wants to leave any money on the table. No one wants to find that she paid more than was necessary, or more than someone else who bought the same product or service. We all want to get the best price, but we know that the lowest price often comes with more problems than we had anticipated.

When you get a last-ditch objection about price, you should look the prospect in the eye and assure her that she is getting a good deal. "Ms. Prospect, this is an excellent price. You are getting a very good deal. When you consider everything that we include in this package, you are going to be very happy with this purchase."

The Just-Suppose Close

You can also use the *just-suppose close*. The prospect says, "I'm sorry, I like what you've shown me, but we've used up our entire budget."

You answer, "Ms. Prospect, just suppose that that was not a problem. Is there any other reason that would cause you to hesitate about going ahead right now?" When you phrase it this way, the prospect has to say, "No, that's the only reason," or "Well, there is another reason."

Whenever you say, "Well, just suppose that's not a problem; suppose we could deal with that to your complete satisfaction; just suppose we could demonstrate that to you conclusively," you can usually uncover the final objection or the closing condition.

"Just suppose we could get the price down by another $100."

"Just suppose I could get approval for this request and get it out for you by Friday."

"Just suppose we could deliver this next week and hold off billing you until your next budget period. Would that work for you?"

The Sharp-Angle Close

You use the *sharp-angle close* to turn an objection into a reason for buying. Sometimes it is called the *bear trap close* or the *porcupine close*. It is very effective when the customer has almost run out of objections or buying resistance. The prospect says, "I can't afford the monthly payments."

You reply, "If we could spread the payments over an extra year and get them down below $400 per month, would you take it?"

The prospect might say, "Your product won't perform to my specifications."

You respond, "If we could demonstrate to you that it will, and give you a guarantee on that, would you take it?"

In other words, use your ability to satisfy the objection as a reason for buying. You close on the objection.

GET THE COMMITMENT FIRST

Inexperienced salespeople often make the mistake of hearing this final objection and then offering to go back to the company to see if they can solve it. The prospect says,

"I like what you've shown me, but I would need it by the end of next week, and you require six weeks for delivery."

Instead of saying, "Let me get back to the office and see if we can't deliver it faster," say, "If we could get it for you by next week, would you take it?"

With the sharp-angle close, the prospect has to either agree to buy your product if you can answer his final condition, or give you the real reason why he is hesitating about going ahead.

"It costs too much." You say, "If we can get you pretty much the same thing for less, will you take it?" The prospect has to say, "Well, if I can get pretty much the same thing at a lower price, I'll take it."

The Instant-Reverse Close

You can use the *instant-reverse close* in a variety of situations. It is a fun close to use and very effective. You can use it on your children and with your spouse. You can use it on both clients and prospects. A friend of mine told me that he doubled his income in less than one year when he started using this close after one of my seminars.

When the prospect gives you any objection at all, especially a standard, well-used objection, such as "We can't afford it," you answer, "Mrs. Prospect, that's *exactly* why you should take it."

This always grabs the prospect's attention and forces her to say, "What? What do you mean?"

Think of a Good Answer

This gives you a few seconds to think up a logical answer to this question.

The prospect says, "It's too expensive."

You reply, "Ms. Prospect, that's exactly why you should take it."

The prospect says, "What do you mean?"

You say, "Ms. Prospect, you want to get this for the lowest possible price, don't you?"

"Of course I do."

"And you want to get the very best quality at the same time, don't you?"

"Well, yes," says the prospect.

"And you're probably going to buy one of these someday anyway, aren't you?"

"Well, yes, probably someday."

"Ms. Prospect, that's exactly why you should take it today at this price, because you'll never get a better combination of product, quality, and price as right now. Why don't you take it?"

Use It Everywhere

One of my clients was with a cable TV company that was selling Pay TV from door to door. The team went out and *tripled* their sales using this single closing technique. The salesperson would knock on the door and ask, "Are you interested in getting Pay Television?" The prospect would immediately say, "No thanks, I can't afford it."

The salesperson would say, "That's exactly why you should take it, Mr. Prospect, *because* you can't afford it."

The door, which was beginning to close, would open up again, and the prospect would say, "What do you mean?"

The reason he hadn't purchased cable or a satellite dish was that, up to now, he had been convinced that he couldn't afford it. The salesperson would say, "Mr. Prospect, may I ask you a question? Are you *ever* going to have Pay TV, with movies, sports, theater, arts, children's programs, and so on, in your home for your family?"

The prospect would say, "Well, yes, someday I will."

"Then that's exactly why you should take it today, Mr. Prospect. Because of this special promotion, you can get it cheaper today than at any other time. There is no hookup fee, and you won't have to start paying until the first of next month. The fact that you don't feel that you can afford it is exactly why you should take it *today*." Homeowners signed up by the hundreds.

TRY IT ON THE TELEPHONE

Sometimes you can use the instant-reverse close while phone prospecting. First, you call up and ask a question aimed at the result or benefit of what you are selling. Or you can ask a question about your product or service and what it can do for the prospect. The prospect mechanically responds, "I'm not interested." You quickly reply by saying, "Mrs. Prospect, I didn't think you'd be interested. That's exactly why I'm calling you."

The prospect says, "What?!"

You say, "Mrs. Prospect, most people using our product were not interested when we first contacted them. The ones who were the least interested turned out to be the most satisfied with what our product does for them. When you say you are not interested, it could mean that this product is exactly what you are looking for. I'd like to get together with you for about ten minutes to show you what we have, and you can decide for yourself. When would be the best time for you?"

Always offer *general* time periods rather than specific times for an appointment. "Would you be available sometime Tuesday morning around ten, or would Wednesday afternoon be better for you?" It is much easier for a prospect to agree to see you on Tuesday morning or sometime Wednesday if you seem open and flexible.

SEMINAR SELLING

A multimillionaire friend of mine who started in sales began conducting free lectures to introduce people to his three-day, wealth-creation seminar. In his talk, he would point out that no one ever got rich working for someone else and that there were several routes to wealth that a person could follow if he learned and practiced them.

Almost consistently, someone in the audience would stand up and say, "Well, I would like to attend, but I can't afford it."

Before learning this instant-reverse close, he would be stumped by this response. But by using the instant-reverse close, he would say, "Sir, that is exactly why you should attend."

By now, everyone in the audience was interested to hear what he was going to say.

He would then ask, "May I ask, how long have you been working since you left high school?"

The audience member would say, "Ten years" or "Twenty years."

The speaker would then say, "This seminar costs $495 for two days, and it is unconditionally guaranteed. You're telling me that you have been out of school and working for ten [or twenty] years, and you still can't afford $495? That is exactly why you should beg, borrow, or steal to come to this seminar to learn how to improve your financial condition so you never have to stand up and say this in a public audience again."

IRRESISTIBLE LOGIC

The answer was so logical that it was almost irresistible. Everyone in the audience who was sitting there thinking that they could not afford to attend the seminar suddenly realized that they had been working for years and they were *still* broke.

If they didn't take this seminar, which was guaranteed anyway, they might still be broke ten years from now. At the end of his lecture, people lined up to enroll in his seminar.

Remember, in using the instant-reverse close, you don't have to have a great follow-up answer. The whole purpose of saying, "That's exactly why you should take it" is to break the prospect's preoccupation. It is to get him to wake up suddenly and pay close attention to you.

The Change-Places Close

Another great close that you can use when you have not been able to uncover the key objection is called the *change-places close*. It is especially effective when the prospect will not give you a straight answer.

This is how it works. You have established a friendly relationship, given your presentation, and the prospect still won't tell you what he is thinking. You say, "Ms. Prospect, let's change places for just a minute. Put yourself in my situation and imagine you were me. Imagine that you are talking to someone whom you respect. You've shown her an excellent product, and yet she won't make a decision one way or another, and she won't give you a reason why. What would you do or say if you were in my shoes?"

Very often, the prospect will identify with you and say, "I understand what you're saying. *This* is my real concern . . ." She will then divulge the real reason she is hesitating about going ahead with your offer.

OFFER A POSSIBLE OBJECTION

If she still won't give you the answer, then you say, "We're really talking about the money, aren't we?" And then wait silently.

The prospect will have to then say either, "Yes, you're right," or "No, it's something else."

When the prospect says, "No, it's not the money," pause and then ask, "Then may I ask what it is?" Again, remain silent.

Eventually the prospect will say, "Well, this is my concern . . ."

You then respond, "Ms. Prospect, if we could handle this concern to your complete satisfaction, would you be prepared to go ahead right now?"

If the prospect agrees, you have made the sale.

Welcome Objections

Objections are a standard and predictable part of any sales conversation. We've all had previous experiences with products and services that were disappointing. We do not want to have those experiences again. Your job is to be patient, polite, and positive, asking good questions and listening intently to the answers. If you are courteous and persistent, eventually the prospect will tell you why he might be hesitating and give you an opportunity to answer his question and close the sale.

Action Exercises:

1. Make a list of every objection that a qualified prospect could give you for not buy what you are selling.

2. Cluster your objections into categories, never more than six, and then develop a powerful, persuasive answer to each one.

3. Use your creativity to find ways to help interested prospects buy your products, in spite of their concerns.

4. Determine the one thing that a prospect must be convinced of to go ahead and buy your product or service; concentrate on finding and proving that he will get this key benefit.

5. Treat every objection as a request for more information, as a need for good reasons to go ahead with the sale.

6. Hear the prospect out completely each time he objects or asks a question; practice all your listening skills.

7. Complete the sentence: "I could sell to everyone I spoke to as long as he didn't say . . ."

Perpetual pushing and assurance put a difficulty out of countenance, and make a seeming difficulty give way.
—Jeremy Collier

4

WINNING CLOSING TECHNIQUES I

The greatest thing in this world is not so much where
we are, but in which direction we are moving.

—Oliver Wendell Holmes Jr.

SELLING IS NOT EASY. EVERY DAY YOU MUST BE UP AND about, prospecting, identifying needs, making presentations, overcoming objections, and closing the sale. It is hard, hard work.

The more ways you know to perform these functions, especially closing the sale, the greater success you will enjoy and the more quickly you will reach the income goals you have set for yourself.

Preparing to Ask for the Order

Before you ask a closing question, be sure that the prospect is ready. Ask a question to ensure that the customer has no lingering queries or objections: "Does this make sense to you, so far?"

If the prospect says, "Yes, this makes sense," you can say, "Well then, how soon do you need it?"

Another question you can ask at the end of your sales presentation is, "Mr. Prospect, do you have any questions or concerns that I haven't covered?"

This is called a *negative answer question*. When the prospect says *no*, he means *yes*. At this point, you can proceed and ask a closing question.

The Ascending Close

One of the best closing techniques you can learn is the *ascending close*, which is sometimes called *the part-by-part close*, or the *automatic close*. This technique involves a series of questions, each of which leads to the next, with all questions requiring a "yes" answer.

For many years, before the Internet came along, the encyclopedia sales presentation was one of the most brilliant ascending close sales methods ever designed. Many people who started their careers selling encyclopedias went on to build successful professions and businesses in other fields with this method and approach to selling.

CAREFULLY CRAFTED QUESTIONS

According to the legend, a group of behavioral psychologists sat down for six weeks and worked together to develop this presentation, word for word. They invested more than $250,000 on the background research and the labor necessary to perfect this process. The encyclopedia presentation consisted of forty-two questions, each requiring a "yes" answer.

The questions would start from the most general to the most specific. Each question would more narrowly qualify the prospect in terms of interest and ability to buy.

For example, the salesperson would knock on the door of the home, either cold-calling or following up on a lead, and the first thing he would say was, "Hello, do you live here?"

It seems like a simple question, but it helped the salesperson immediately determine whether or not he should proceed with the presentation. If the person who answered the door was merely a visitor, he would ask if he could speak to the person who actually lived in the apartment or home.

ASK EASY QUESTIONS

The second question would be, "We are doing a survey in this neighborhood for a national educational organization; may I ask you a couple of questions?"

Almost invariably, the prospect would say yes. People love to give their opinions.

The salesperson would then ask, "Do you believe in the importance of education?"

The prospect would predictably answer yes once more. The salesperson has now asked three "yes" questions. "Do you live here? Would you answer a couple of questions for our survey? Do you believe in the value of higher education?"

"May I come in?" Answer: "Yes."

"May I sit down?" Answer: "Yes."

"As part of our public relations program, we will be placing a set of encyclopedias in a few selected homes in this neighborhood at no charge. Would this be of interest to you and your family?"

Again, the prospect would answer yes. Everyone likes the idea of getting something free.

The salesperson would say, "We don't sell these encyclopedias. What we do is place them in your living room so that when your neighbors visit and see them and ask where you got them, you tell them that you got them from us and refer them to us, so that we can come by and show them how they can get these encyclopedias for their homes as well. Would you do that?" And again, the answer is yes.

Each Question in Order

This ascending close presentation marched through forty-two questions, each of which required a yes answer for the salesperson to proceed. If ever the prospect said no, the sales conversation would come to an end.

By the end of the presentation, which started off with the offer of a free set of encyclopedias as a public relations gesture, the prospect would have purchased a $3,000 set of encyclopedias, signed up for the yearbook for ten years, and received a free globe, bookcase, and set of sports and children's encyclopedias. He would have written a check for a $500 deposit, signed a one-year payment plan, and would be looking forward to all the educational books that he would soon have in his home.

THE POWER OF YES

The reason the ascending close presentation is so effective is that it is based on the suggestive power of affirmative answers.

When you ask a series of six or more questions to which the prospect says yes, the prospect will thereafter nod and agree with almost anything you say.

If you can ask six "yes" questions at the beginning of your

If you can ask six "yes" questions at the beginning of your presentation, it becomes very hard for a normal person to say no later on.

presentation, it becomes very hard for a normal person to say no later on. If you can ask six questions that require a "yes" answer to the benefits that your product or service offers, the prospect will often be completely convinced of the goodness and value of your offer.

REPHRASE THE SAME QUESTION

You can often ask the *same question* with slightly different words. For example:

"Mrs. Prospect, would you like to increase your profits?" Answer: "Yes."

"Are you interested in cutting your costs?" Answer: "Yes."

"Would you like to operate your business more efficiently?" Answer: "Yes."

"Would you like to get more done in less time?" Answer: "Yes."

"Would you be interested in a cost-effective method that more than pays for itself over time?" Answer: "Yes."

"Would you like to get started with this right away?" Answer: "Yes."

OFFER THE SAME BENEFIT

When the prospect says yes six times in a row, she will respond positively to almost anything you say, even if the questions are the same benefit, just phrased differently:

"Is one of your goals financial independence?"

"Would you like to earn the highest return possible with minimum risk?"

"Would you like to earn a much higher return than you would get from a savings account or money market fund?"

"Would you like to see an investment that is the favorite investment vehicle for thousands of sophisticated investors like yourself?"

"If you found something that gave you all these benefits, would you want to get started with it right away?"

Every time you ask a question, the *interest* of the prospect goes up. Every yes increases the *desire* for what you are selling. Every time you ask a "yes" question, you are throwing fuel on the fire and intensifying the emotion of the prospect.

Choose Your Words Carefully

On the other hand, every no *decreases* buying desire. It is like throwing water on the fire. This is why it is important that you structure each question so that the only answer you get from a qualified prospect is affirmative. They must answer yes.

Properly designed and practiced, the ascending close is one of the most powerful ways of selling ever developed. It is used successfully to sell investments, life insurance, professional services, educational products, software, computers, high tech of all kinds, and many other things. Even vacuum cleaners and home repairs are sold using the ascending close presentation.

When you ask enough "yes" questions, starting from the general to the particular, moving logically from one point to the next, the prospect's buying desire mounts and mounts. Finally, at a certain point, he will burst out with, "I'll take it. How much is it? How soon can I get it? Where do I sign?"

Building Buying Desire

Each time you describe a *benefit* in a sales presentation, purchasing desire increases. Here is an example. Imagine a friend was describing a new restaurant to you.

"I'd like to tell you about a new restaurant I went to. First of all, the *food is fabulous.* They have a *great wine list,* and the *prices are very reasonable.* The *decor is beautiful,* with *classical music* playing and a pianist in the main dining room. The *service is incredible*. The manager is a *really nice guy*, and everyone, including the waiters, *treats you as if you owned the restaurant*. There is lots of *free parking* right next to the restaurant, and it's *not even crowded* yet, because not too many people know about it."

As your friend describes all the desirable features of the restaurant, your desire to go there as soon as possible increases dramatically. Soon you can hardly wait to get to a telephone and make a reservation.

DESCRIBE THE BENEFITS

When you are describing the benefits of your product or service to your prospect, and you are positive and animated, eventually the prospect reaches the point where he says, "How soon can I get this?"

The more logical and preplanned your ascending-close presentation, the faster and easier you will be able to sell. It takes a little work to design and perfect such a presentation, but once you have it perfected, it is almost irresistible.

The Invitational Close

The *invitational close* is one of the most influential techniques used in modern selling. At the end of your sales presentation, you simply issue a direct invitation to buy what you have just described.

In its simplest form, you first of all ask, "Do you like what I have shown you so far?"

When the prospect says, "Yes, it looks pretty good," you immediately go into an invitational close and ask, "Well then, why don't you give it a try?"

When you encourage a person to "give it a try," it sounds like an easy decision to make. Prospects who are reluctant to *buy* the product are often at least willing to "give it a try." Your job is to issue him an invitation.

UNCOVER LINGERING OBJECTIONS

Occasionally, when you say, "Why don't you give it a try?" the prospect will think of a reason that might be causing her to hesitate. Simply slow down, answer the objection clearly, and ask, "Does that answer your question?" Then proceed to ask her to buy once more.

If you are selling services, ask, "Why don't you give *us* a try?" When you use the word *us* in this question, it implies that your entire organization will wrap its arms around the customer and work to ensure that he or she is satisfied.

If you are selling services, ask, "Why don't you give us a try?" When you use the word us in this question, it implies that your entire organization will wrap its arms around the customer and work to ensure that he or she is satisfied.

If you are selling a tangible product, like a car or a refrigerator, you can use the invitational close by saying, "Why don't you take it?" or "Why don't you buy it?"

JUST ASK

Even if the prospect is saying things like, "I'm not sure, maybe I should wait until later," or "I don't know if I can afford it; let me think it over," you can say, "Yes, I know all that. But it's a superior product at a good price. Why don't you just take it?" And then remain perfectly silent. You will be amazed at how many customers have run completely out of sales resistance by this time. They are just waiting for you to invite them to make a buying decision. When you do, they are almost relieved. They will often say, "Oh, all right, I'll take it."

SEVERAL WAYS TO ASK

Some of the standard invitational closing questions are:

"When would you like delivery?"

"How soon do you need it?"

"Would you like to have this sent to your home or your office address?"

"Which color would you prefer?"

"Which size do you prefer?"

"When would you like to get started?"

"Do you need this right away?"

In every case, when you use an invitational close, the prospect must either agree and go along with you while you wrap up the sale or give you an objection that you are prepared to answer with something like, "How do you mean exactly?"

By using the invitational close, you keep control of the sales conversation. "Are you in a rush, or would Tuesday be all right?" If the prospect says, "Tuesday would be good," you have made the sale.

Dealing with Price Resistance

We talked before about price resistance. Everyone has problems with price. These price concerns often go back to early childhood, to all the emotional issues surrounding money that you have dealt with all your life. The good news is that price is seldom the reason for buying or not buying a product or service. Price is important, but there is almost always something else that is *more* important.

POINTS TO REMEMBER ABOUT PRICE

1. No one can afford it. No one can ever afford the price the first time it comes up. No matter what the price, it usually costs too much, more than the prospect expected to pay. More often than not, this is either because the prospect had no idea going in what it would cost or he has not budgeted for it.

Not long ago, we were promoting a two-day, weekend seminar. From the stage, I said, "This seminar is only *four-ninety-five* per person." Many people went immediately to the back of the room or phoned us later and said they wanted to go to the seminar that was only $4.95 for the weekend, all inclusive. Instead of 495 *dollars*, they thought that we were talking about *four dollars and ninety-five cents*. And even then, they asked for a discount. They had no idea how much it cost to put on a two-day seminar in a first-class hotel or convention center, and as a result, they were shocked when they heard the real price. This is quite common.

The fact is that the amount of money that anyone has is *limited*. When you give a price, this amount represents all of the other things that the prospect could buy with the same amount of money. This is called the *principle of the excluded alternative*. Every choice implies the *exclusion* of something else. For everything you buy, there is something else that you *cannot* buy.

Each person values the freedom of choice very highly. When you buy something, you give up a certain amount of choice. You limit your options because you reduce the amount of money that you have available. This is why, when price comes up, no matter what it is, people automatically say, "I can't afford it."

When you first tell your prospect what the product is going to cost, he will be surprised. This is why you must spend a good deal of time building the value of your product or service before you ever mention price for the first time.

2. Willingness and ability are different. *Willingness* to pay and *ability* to pay are two different things. No one is ever willing to pay any price that you ask. No one ever wants to part with her money and thereby cut off her options.

But whether one can *afford* to pay is a totally different issue. Most people can buy a product or service if they want it badly enough. Your goal is to increase the willingness to pay by building buying desire. Repeating and emphasizing the benefits that your prospect will enjoy from your product or service will accomplish this goal. The more the prospect wants what you are selling, the less sensitive she will be to the price.

Convince the prospect that the *value* of your product is far *greater* than the cost. She must be fully persuaded that the advantages she will receive are vastly greater than the money you are asking.

Put off the discussion of price whenever you can possibly avoid it. Instead, talk about benefits. When you come to the price later, it will not seem as high.

3. Price out of place kills the sale. That is a fundamental rule in selling. If you bring up the issue of price before the prospect has decided that he wants to own and enjoy your product or service, he will lose interest, and the conversation will be over.

Often the prospect will ask *at the beginning* of a sales conversation, "How much is it?" At this stage, he has no earthly idea what you are even selling. He has no understanding of the features and benefits you offer or how much better off he would be by owning what you sell. If you give the price *before* the prospect knows these things, he will have nothing to relate it to. The price will then become the most important issue in the conversation, and he will predictably state, "That's too much; I can't afford it."

LOSING THE SALE

When the prospect says, "Just tell me the price, and I will tell you if I am interested," he is attempting to speed up the information process and shorten the conversation. If you answer this question now, you will kill the sale.

He has no value to compare your price against, no clue what he gets for the money. When you put the price out in front of the prospect, all alone, before you have presented values or benefits to offset it, the prospect has no choice but to say that it costs too much.

Sidestep the Price Question

When I was telephone prospecting, I found that there is an expression that is common to virtually all buyers in America. It is the words *how much is it*, compressed into a single phrase: *"Howmuchisit?"*

When I was starting out, I often gave the price just to get the prospect to listen to me. But as sure as I did, I would hear, "I'm not interested." *Slam!* And she would hang up on me.

I soon learned that if I gave the price before I had a chance to give a presentation, I would not even get to first base. I therefore developed an alternative way of handling this question on the phone.

"How much is it?" says the predictable prospect.

"Ms. Prospect, that's the *best part!*" I would reply cheerily. "If it is not *just right* for you, there's no charge."

"What do you mean?" (Again, as predicted.)

I would then say, "Ms. Prospect, what I'm calling you about, if it's not *exactly* right for you, you are not going to take it, are you?"

The prospect would say, "No, I'm not."

"Well then, Ms. Prospect, if you don't take it, then there's no charge."

This would always trigger the words, "Oh. Well then, what is it?"

"That's what I'd like to talk to you about. I just need ten minutes of your time; I have something I have to *show* you." I would then go on to arrange a ten-minute, face-to-face appointment with the prospect.

THE COMMON DENOMINATOR

There is a reason that people ask for the price at the very beginning. It is because money is the common denominator in our society. The *monetary unit*, whether it be the dollar, the euro, or the franc, is standard across all transactions. We relate to products and services by finding out how much they cost. The cost tells us where the product or service exists in our universe. We ask the price so that we can *fit* a particular product or service into our world of experience.

Why do you think people talk about the weather? It is because everyone can relate to the weather. It is another common denominator in our society. It affects everybody in the same way. Asking the price of anything is just like commenting on the weather. But *you must avoid the question* if it arises too early in the sales conversation.

THE REASON FOR PRICE RESISTANCE

Price resistance is how a prospect tells you that you have not given him enough evidence that the benefits outweigh the price. For this reason, never argue about price. Never say that your price is "good" or "reasonable" or "fair," or anything else. Whatever the prospect says about your price, *agree*. Then go on to say something like, "Mr. Prospect, this product is definitely not cheap. However, there are good reasons for why it costs what it does. Let me explain to you why we charge what we do." Or "There are good reasons why thousands of people like you have examined this product carefully, compared it with our competitors, and decided to pay more for it, even when they knew they could get something similar for less. Would you like to know what they are?"

BE PROUD OF YOUR PRICES

If you charge a high price, be proud of it. If the prospect says, "That's sure expensive!" you say, "Yes, Mr. Prospect. In fact, we are the highest-price supplier of this product in this market. And we are selling more of this today than ever before. Would you like to know why so many people are buying our products and using our services even though we charge more?" You will usually get a yes to this, and a chance to explain why your product or service is as good as it is.

DIMINISHING PRICE RESISTANCE

Here is a common experience. A woman goes into a swanky retail store or boutique, looks at a dress, and sees that the price tag is $800. She says, "My, that's a lot of money."

The sales associate agrees and says, "Yes, this is an expensive dress. It's a St. John's Knit. There is a good reason why they charge so much for this. First of all, it is made from the finest materials, hand stitched, with beautiful buttons, collars, and lining. When you wear it, you feel as if you are one of the most expensively dressed women in America. It holds its value. It is timeless in terms of tailoring. You can wear it year after year, and it always looks great. *This* is why it costs $800."

When a potential buyer learns all the reasons that a particular product is as expensive as it is, her price resistance declines as her buying desire increases. That's why countless hundreds of millions of dollars of high-fashion clothes are sold every year. It is because of the focus on value rather than price.

> *If you charge a high price, be proud of it.*

Always justify the price with sound reasons. Explain carefully why it costs as much as it does. Never discuss price without mentioning the value and benefits of your offering at the same time.

PUT OFF PRICE UNTIL LATER

Let me reemphasize: *do not bring up price at the beginning of your talk, under any conditions.* When a prospect says, "Well, that looks very interesting; how much is it?" you reply, "Good question. Can I come back to that in a minute?" or "The price is the *best* part. I'm going to come to it in just a minute, and you're going to be very pleased when you hear it. But *before I do*, may I ask you a couple of questions?" Then go on to ask questions and take control of the sales conversation.

CHOOSE YOUR TIMING

In my sales presentations, I always have a specific point at which I explain price for the first time. By that point in the conversation, the customer fully understands what I am selling and why it is the best choice for him, right now. Only then do I say, "I'll bet you would like to know how much this is going to cost."

You must increase her buying desire by emphasizing results and benefits. You do not increase buying desire by arguing about the price

But price does not come up until that point. I don't mention it until *I* decide that it is appropriate to bring it up. If the price question comes up earlier, I put it off.

To reduce price sensitivity, continually focus your presentation on the value received rather than on the money charged. Talk about what the product does for the customer instead of its cost.

The Sandwich Close

When the time has finally come to address the question of price, don't simply tell a prospect a certain number of dollars. Instead you use what is called a *sandwich close.*

With this close, you sandwich the price between two descriptions of the value and benefits the customer will enjoy with this product. For example, "This machine, including these benefits and features, plus these attachments, a supply of basic materials and fuel, *and* a ninety-day warranty, will cost you X number of dollars per month once it is in operation. Not only that, we provide complete training and customer support for you until we are sure that you are getting maximum value from this product."

In this case, you are sandwiching the price in between two descriptions of customer benefits. This descriptions of benefits keeps the customer focused on the value she receives rather than its cost.

Here is an important rule in selling: *increased buying desire reduces price sensitivity.* The more the prospect wants what you are selling, the less concerned she will be about the price. You must increase her buying desire by emphasizing results and benefits. You do not increase buying desire by arguing about the price.

Compare Your Prices with Those of Your Competitors

You can minimize price resistance by comparing the price with more expensive articles. When a prospect says, "It costs too much," you can answer with, "Compared with what, Mr. Prospect?" Often he has no idea what he is talking about. He knows nothing of your product, or of products similar to yours. He may have never bought one of your products, or has not bought one for several years. He doesn't realize that prices may have gone up substantially since his last purchase.

When you ask, "Compared with what?" the prospect could say, "Well, compared with ABC's product, yours seems expensive."

You reply, "As it happens, ABC's product, which is similar to ours but lacking certain features and benefits, costs $275 more than ours does. As a matter of fact, here's their recent price sheet." *Show* the prospect written price comparisons. Logic does make sales. Give the prospect the evidence that he needs to feel confident in proceeding with your offer.

COMPARE APPLES TO APPLES

It's essential that you find out what prospects are comparing you with. For instance, if you say, "This Mercedes costs $105,000," and they say, "Wow! That's a lot," you then ask, "Compared with what?" If they are comparing your Mercedes to a Honda, yes, your Mercedes costs a lot more. But there are very distinct reasons a Mercedes is more expensive than a Honda. "Would you like to know what they are?"

Always compare apples to apples and oranges to oranges. Find out what your competitors are charging for what you sell, and the reasons for any price differential.

When a prospect says, "That seems awfully expensive," you can say, "Mr. Prospect, here are our major competitors. These are the products they offer, and this is what they are asking for them. You can see that, in comparison with these other suppliers, our products are very fairly priced."

Stretch It over the Life of the Product

You can reduce price resistance by stretching the price over the life of the product. If the prospect feels that your price tag is too high, you can point out that it costs $300 more than the competitive offering, but your machine has a five-year life.

"Even though you pay $300 more," you can reason, "it works out to about $60 per year, which is about $2 a month more for all of the additional quality, features, benefits, and accessories that are built into our product. Is it worth $2 more, or six cents a day, for you to have the best product of its kind on the market?"

Business Is Bad

Sometimes people say, "Business is bad." Even in boom times, folks complain that business is not as good as they expected and that they don't have enough cash. The reason for this is that during the slow times in business, people become accustomed to complaining about how bad business is. When business is booming, they retain the habit and continue to complain, even though their complaints are no longer valid.

When a prospect says that she cannot buy at this time because business is bad, it simply means that you haven't given her enough reasons to buy. You have not aroused enough buying desire. Keep focusing on the results and benefits of your product, of what it does for your prospect, and how it improves her life and work. Intensified buying desire reduces price sensitivity.

Offer Alternatives

Sometimes prospects will say they are "short of cash." In response you can ask, "What if we could offer you terms, and you could pay if off over an extended period of time?" Or try these:

"What if we could take your existing product as a trade so that you need no cash to begin using our new product?"

"What if we could delay payments until your next budget period?"

"What if we could extend payments over a five-year period rather than a three-year period, thereby lowering the monthly payments?"

When the prospect brightens up and becomes interested in your counteroffers, it means that he is capable of buying; he is just looking for a way to make it work. This is where you use your creativity at its highest level.

Buying a Mercedes

Some years ago, I saw a successful businessman my age driving a silver-grey Mercedes Benz 450 SEL four-door sedan, with blue leather upholstery. From that moment on, all I could think about was owning such a beautiful car.

One day I was calling on a car dealership. In the middle of the conversation, the general manager said to me, "I have the perfect car for you. Come over here and look out the window." Just below the second-story window was a silver-grey Mercedes 450 SEL sedan. It was my dream car in every respect. But my first reaction was typical of most buyers. "Sorry, I'm not in the market. I can't afford it. It costs too much. It looks great, but it's not for me."

FIND A WAY TO MAKE IT WORK

But the general manager had cut his teeth in car sales. He was a consummate professional. He said, "You may be right. It may be the wrong car for you at this time. But what if we could take your existing car as a trade-in so that there would be no cash out of your pocket at all to drive away in that car?"

My heart leaped in my throat. "Well," I said, "I couldn't afford it."

He then said, "Brian, what if we could finance the whole purchase for you?"

When he calculated the monthly payments, I replied, "I can't afford that much each month."

He replied, "Because this is a Mercedes, we can stretch the monthly payments over five years rather than three. Could you afford that?"

I never had a chance. They took my car in trade for the full down payment. They financed the balance of the cost through one of their own banks and spread the payments over five years. Because I bought it through my company, I was able to write off the interest and depreciation. My cost out of pocket for the Mercedes came out to only $125 per month. It was one of the most beautiful cars I ever owned.

My point is that there is always a way to make a deal

work if the prospect wants the product badly enough. You have to be creative. Once your prospect has expressed an intense interest to own and enjoy what you are selling, *find* ways to make it work for him.

Dealing with Budget Limitations

Prospects often resist buying because of "budget limitations." The prospect says, "We don't have it in the budget. Our budget is all used up."

You can counter with, "Here is a solution. We will sell you the product now, but we won't send you the bill until your next budget period. How does that sound?"

If the customer really wants it, she'll almost without fail agree. As an alternative, you can take something else in trade, or a minimal down payment, or offer a cheaper product that does the same thing, or even try to get the customer's budget expanded to include your product at this time. Find a way.

You Get What You Pay For

From time to time, when the price is above the customer's expectations, he will say, "That's more than we expected to pay. Can't I get it for less?"

Here is how you respond. First, you ask, "Mr. Prospect, did you ever get something for nothing?"

He will admit that he never really got something for nothing.

WINNING CLOSING TECHNIQUES I | 127

You then ask, "Mr. Prospect, did you ever get anything cheap that turned out to be any good?"

Again, after a few seconds, he will concede that he never got anything cheap that turned out to be of any value.

Finally, you ask, "Mr. Prospect, isn't it true that you always get pretty much what you pay for?"

When he agrees that this is true, you can then say, "Mr. Prospect, this is a great price, and this is a very competitive market. We are selling this product for the lowest possible price we can and still stay in business. If you want a

Never forget that, in the eyes of a customer, salespersons' assertions are not proof. Just because you say something is true does not mean that it is true in the mind of the prospect.

great-quality product that is going to last a long time and do the job for you, sometimes you have to flex your budget somewhere else to get the money you need. Isn't that true?"

Salespersons' Assertions Are Not Proof

Never forget that, in the eyes of a customer, salespersons' assertions are not proof. Just because *you* say something is true does not mean that it is true in the mind of the prospect. *You* know that you would never lie, but nobody else knows that. Customers are accustomed to believing that you will put the very best light on your product and that you will even exaggerate the benefits of your product if that's what it takes to get the sale.

When you say to a customer, "This is very competitively priced," it doesn't mean a thing. But when you present a price comparison from a recent newspaper or magazine or a price list from your major competitor, this is accepted as valid evidence.

When you say, "You'll be very happy with this product," the prospect may say, "Yes, I'm sure I would." But she will be skeptical. However, if you can back up your statement with a testimonial letter from one of your happy customers, that letter is considered conclusive proof.

Lowest Common Denominator

You can reduce price resistance by breaking the price down to its lowest common denominator. Compare the price of your product with a Coca-Cola or cup of coffee. Some people compare their products to a bottle of wine or a case of beer per week. Some compare it with a dinner out one night per month. Compare your price to something that your prospect consumes on a regular basis.

The Ultimatum Close

A source of great frustration in selling is when prospects procrastinate on the buying decision. You will continually deal with customers who drag their feet. They won't say yes, and they won't say no. They are "thinking about it." They are talking it over with someone. They are reviewing it with their accountant, and so on.

This can become a real problem. You have now invested many hours in calling on this prospect, and calling back. You don't want to lose your entire investment, but you are not making the sale and you are not earning any commissions. What do you do?

In this case, you can use the *ultimatum close*. Sometimes it is called the *end of the trail close* or the *sudden death close*. It enables you to take control of the process and resolve the sale, one way or the other.

FISH OR CUT BAIT

Here's how it works. First, fill out the sales contract, exactly the way you have discussed it in the past. Then call the prospect and tell him that you need to see him about something that has come up. You have been there so many times that he will almost without a doubt agree to see you.

When you sit down with the prospect, look him in the eye and say these words: "Mr. Prospect, I have given this a lot of thought, and either this is a good idea for you, or it's not. But one way or another, let's make a decision right now. What do you say?

"I've filled out this contract exactly the way we've discussed it, and if you'll just authorize it, we can get started on it right away."

You take the completed sales contract, put a tick mark by

the signature line, put your pen on top of the contract, and push it over to the prospect. Then remain perfectly silent and wait.

According to studies on the use of this closing technique, 59 percent of prospects will look at your contract, look back at you, look back at the contract, and eventually sign it. The sale will be made. The other 41 percent of prospects will go through the same process and then push it away and decide not to buy. But in either case, you will now be free to get on with the rest of your sales career.

Bridge the Gap

Sometimes the best answer when a prospect says, "That is more than I expected to pay," is, "Mr. Prospect, *how far apart are we?*"

Or you can ask, "Mr. Prospect, what do we have to do to make a deal today? You tell me the very most you can afford to pay, and I will tell you, one way or another, whether or not we can make this work."

In many cases, you are not far apart. The sale could be just within your reach. But you must know the number that is going around in the customer's mind. Often, customers cannot emotionally pay any more than the number that they have settled on. You must find out what it is.

A SMALL DIFFERENCE
One of my students was a landscape architect. He was invited to submit a proposal to a homebuilder to do the

landscaping for a new home. The contractor told him that he wanted the very lowest price possible. The landscape architect really wanted the work, so he sat down and put together a very tight proposal. He complied with all the specifications of the contractor and put in his bid for $7,025.

The contractor became very emotional. He blew up and said, "Absolutely not! It's too much. It's far beyond what I expected to pay." He rejected the proposal and slammed down the phone.

My student asked for my advice. I told him to go to the phone, call the contractor, and ask, "How far apart are we?"

At the break in the seminar, he went and did this. He came back with a big smile on his face. The contractor had budgeted exactly $7,000 for this job. My student was only $25 out of the ballpark. He quickly adjusted the size of a couple of the plants in his proposal, rewrote the bid, and got the contract the next day.

How Important Is Price?

We've already mentioned the customer's attempt to shorten the sales conversation. He says, "Just tell me how much it costs, and I'll tell you if I'm interested."

Here's a good response: "Mr. Prospect, *is price your only concern?* Are you going to make a buying decision on something as important as this solely on the basis of the cheapest price?"

When you put it like this, almost all prospects will answer no.

You continue with, "I know price is important to you, but so are quality, guarantees, warranties, delivery, and follow-up service. We may not be able to give you the lowest *price*, but we can give you the very *best deal* on the market today, of which price is only a part. How does that sound to you?"

Your willingness and ability to ask for the reasons behind customer hesitation will open every door for you. Your readiness to ask for the sale whenever you see an opportunity will move you into the top 10 percent in your field. The arts of answering objections and closing sales are essential selling skills that you can learn and perfect with time and practice.

Action Exercises:

1. Make a list of all the variations you get on price objections; design an answer for each one so that you are ready when it comes up.

2. Stretch the price of what you sell over the life of the product or service; what does it cost per day, and what else costs the same amount?

3. Select a prospect you have seen several times who will not give you a yes or no answer; go back to him or her and try out the ultimatum close.

4. Determine the key benefits that your customer gets

when he buys your product, and then think of ways to emphasize them whenever price resistance occurs.

5. Design an ascending close presentation for what you sell; write out a series of "yes" questions that you can ask, moving from the general to the particular.

6. Be prepared to back up everything you say to arouse desire and answer objections; refuse to rely on positive assertions that the prospect may discount.

7. Use your creativity to find ways around objections that block the sale; there is almost always a solution.

Patience and perseverance have a magical effect before which difficulties disappear and obstacles vanish.
—John Quincy Adams

5

WINNING CLOSING TECHNIQUES II

The operative assumption is that someone, somewhere, has a
better idea; and the operative compulsion is to find out who
has that better idea, learn it, and put it into action fast.

—Jack Welch

IN GOLF THERE IS A SAYING: "YOU DRIVE FOR SHOW, BUT
you putt for dough."

In selling, you must prospect, identify needs, present solu-
tions, and answer objections. This is the "drive" part of selling.
But it is only when you can step up to the plate, ask for the
order, and close the sale that you actually make the "dough."

Throughout sales history, merchants have used a variety
of ways to help a customer make a buying decision. The
closing techniques that we have discussed up to now, and

those to come, are some of the simplest, most popular, and most powerful closing techniques ever developed. It is up to you to think them through and determine how you can use each one to sell more of your products or services.

Just as a great cook has mastered a large variety of recipes for different dishes, it is essential that you master a variety of closing techniques. You should be able to ask for the order at least ten different ways, depending upon the type of person you are selling to and the kind of objections you receive.

The Secondary Close

The *secondary close*, which is both easy to use and well-liked, involves your closing on a *minor point* in the sales presentation. If the prospect agrees to the minor point, he has, by extension, decided to buy the entire offer.

For example, if a person is considering buying a car, a refrigerator, a stove, or some other consumer durable, use a secondary close by asking, "Would you prefer this in blue or green?"

The color is a secondary issue. The purchase is the major issue. If the prospect says that he would prefer it in blue, he has decided to buy the entire product.

ASK ABOUT DELIVERY

Another way to use the secondary close is to ask, "Would you like this delivered, or would you rather take it with you today?"

How the prospect takes delivery is the secondary issue.

But by saying that he wants to take it with him today, he has made the decision to buy.

The secondary close is not a form of manipulation. Professional salespeople do not use tricks, games, or manipulation in the sales process. The secondary close merely helps the customer through the moment of indecision and stress that always accompanies a buying decision. By getting the prospect focused on a secondary issue, you make it easier for the prospect to make a buying decision. This is beneficial to both of you.

OFFER A CHOICE

If the prospect is thinking of buying a car and cannot make up his mind, you could ask, "By the way, would you want this with the factory tires, or would you prefer Michelin radials?"

If the prospect says, "I would want the radial tires," she has come to a decision.

You then say, "Well then, let's get this written up and get the tires installed so that you can drive it away."

Once the pressure of the buying decision has passed, which is achieved by focusing the prospect on the secondary issue, you simply go on to write up the details.

The Alternative Close

The *alternative close* is also helpful in overcoming the stress of making a buying decision. You can use it in a variety of ways. It involves giving a customer a choice between something and something *else*, rather than a choice between something and nothing.

Customers today are highly individualistic. They prefer to have *choices* rather than ultimatums. Instead of offering one product and asking, "Would you like to buy this?" offer an alternative way of buying the same product.

"Would you prefer the red one or the blue one?"

"Would you rather take the large or the medium size?"

"Would you like the deluxe or the regular?"

Whichever the prospect chooses, he has made a buying decision.

OFFER PAYMENT OR DELIVERY CHOICES

If your product only offers a single choice, present an alternative method of payment or delivery. If you are selling a refrigerator, and the refrigerator *only* comes in white, say, "Do you need this delivered this week, or could we deliver it to you next week?" That way the customer is still being offered a *choice*.

If you are selling an intangible, such as a life insurance policy, you could ask, "Would you want this correspondence sent to your home address or to your office?"

Whichever the customer chooses, the sale is closed.

The Assumption Close

The *assumption close* is a powerful way to maintain control of the sales process. Begin by asking a confirming question, such as, "Does this make sense to you so far?"

WINNING CLOSING TECHNIQUES II | 139

If the prospect says, "Yes, that sounds pretty good," you then assume that the prospect has said yes to the sale. This is very important. You must *act* as if he has just said, "I'll take it. What is the next step?"

"Well then, the next step is this . . ." Go on to describe the *plan of action*, what happens now. Take out your purchase order, contract, or agreement, and begin filling it out. "I will need your OK on this form. We will need a check for $1,250, and we will have this out to you by next Wednesday. How does that sound?" The prospect will almost always agree with you as you write up the paperwork. Wrap up the transaction quickly.

KEEP CONTROL OF THE SALE

The power of the assumption close is that it enables you to keep control of the transaction. Once you've said, "Then the next step is this," and have described the plan of action, the prospect has to either go along with you or give you another objection, which you are quite prepared to answer.

This is often called *selling past the sale*. Instead of discussing the purchase any further, you begin talking about ownership and enjoyment. You direct the prospect's attention toward taking possession of the product and what will happen at that time. The prospect's focus is taken away from saying yes or no and is focused on payment and delivery.

SELL PAST THE SALE

One way to sell past the sale is by asking, "Would you like this gift wrapped?" Or ask, "Would you like to pay for this with cash or a credit card?" Either question gives the prospect a chance to say yes to one of your proposed choices and allows you to close the sale smoothly.

ASK FOR THE DATE OR ADDRESS

A simple way to use the assumption close at the end of a presentation is by pulling out your pen, glancing briefly at the prospect, and asking, "What is your correct mailing address?" Then pose over the sales contract, prepared to write it down.

You will notice in a movie or a stage play that the conclusion is very carefully planned. It is not left to chance. It does not simply "happen" toward the end of the show. It is deliberately designed for maximum impact at exactly the right moment.

By the same token, you must plan your method of closing the same way. When you come to the close, you must know exactly what you are going to do and then just switch into the close exactly as you would shift gears in your car as you drove down the street.

The Take-Away Close

The *take-away close* is a powerful way of getting the vacillating prospect to make a decision. It is a variation of the "selling past the sale close," or the "assumption close."

When the prospect has heard your presentation and obviously likes your offer, but cannot seem to make a decision, you preemptively halt the presentation and say, "Oh, just a minute. Before we go any further, let me check and make sure that we still have this product available in our warehouse."

In retail settings, the clerk will often say, "Let me check and make sure that we have this in your size [or in that color]."

If the prospect allows you to phone the warehouse or go back into the stockroom to see if the item is still in stock

> *When you come to the close, you must know exactly what you are going to do and then just switch into the close exactly as you would shift gears in your car as you drove down the street.*

or if they have the right size or color, she has unconsciously decided to buy. Once you confirm that the item is available, immediately assume the sale and begin filling out the order form.

Go and Check with Another Person

A variation of the take-away close is when you stop at the end of the presentation and say, "Let me check with my manager and see if we can arrange immediate delivery. Can you wait here for a second?"

If the prospect says, "Sure, go ahead," the decision is already made.

You can make this even more impactful by saying, "Why don't you *come with me* to see my manager, and let's see if we can't . . ." If the prospect gets up and follows you, he plans to buy.

SHOPPING FOR CLOTHES

The take-away close is used on people all the time, especially when they are shopping for clothes. The person is looking at an article of clothing, but can't seem to make up his or her mind one way or the other. The salesperson then says, "Just a minute. Before we go any further, let me check and make sure we have it in your size."

In selling hard goods, especially cars, the salesperson will often say, "We are almost sold out of this model; it is so popular. Let me check and make sure we can get this model in the color you want. Can you wait here for a second?"

If the prospect says, "Yes, by all means," she has made up her mind to buy the car if you have it or can get it.

THE TAKE-AWAY TRIGGERS ACTION

Sometime ago, I was selling my house. The economy was soft, and the number of buyers able to purchase a house in that price range was limited. I was asking $275,000.

I got an offer for $240,000. The prospective purchaser thought he could get my house at a lower price because of the softness of the market.

Just before I had to make a decision on whether or not to accept his price, another prospective buyer appeared. Before he had even seen my house, the new client said that if he liked it, he would make an offer immediately.

We went back to the first purchaser and made a counter-offer of $255,000. We told him that we had a second buyer coming to see the house, and if this first buyer did not agree to the counteroffer, we would sell it immediately to the other buyer at the higher offer that we expected to get.

The night before the second buyer saw the house, the first prospective buyer phoned up and closed the deal at $255,000. It turned out later that the second buyer wasn't willing to pay that much, but the thought of losing the sale, having it taken away, triggered the first buyer into raising his offer and closing the deal. This sort of sale takes place all the time.

Sometimes people do not know how much they want a product or service until you suggest that they may not be able to get it. At times, it is only when you threaten to take it away that they step up and make a buying decision.

Sometimes people do not know how much they want a product or service until you suggest that they may not be able to get it. At times, it is only when you threaten to take it away that they step up and make a buying decision.

The Summary Close

When there are several features and benefits included in your offering, you can try the *summary close*. Here's how. When you get to the end of your sales presentation, say, "Well, we've covered a lot of information. Let me just summarize some of these things for you, and then you can make a decision one way or the other. OK?"

Remember, features arouse interest, but *benefits arouse buying desire.* Each time you repeat a benefit that is meaningful to the prospect, his buying desire heightens. If you describe enough benefits, all in a row, the individual's buying desire shoots up, often to the point where he will spontaneously say, "I'll take it. How soon can I get it?"

To use the summary close, go through each feature and benefit, one at a time, and repeat what the customer gets with each one. Each time you itemize a feature and point out the benefit that the customer will enjoy, his desire to own your product or service grows.

If you are planning to use the summary close, make up a list, in advance, of the most attractive features of your product, and rank them in order of importance. Plan your presentation to introduce them in order. Watch the prospect for the one or two benefits that seem to be of greatest interest to him, and then emphasize them repeatedly throughout the presentation.

At the end of the summary close, the prospect's buying desire will be at its peak. You then ask, "Have I covered everything?"

If the prospect says yes, simply assume the sale by asking, "How soon would you need this?"

The Puppy-Dog Close

This is one of the most popular of all closing techniques. It is used to sell billions of dollars' worth of products each year. It is based on letting the prospect touch, taste, feel, hold, or try out the product or service.

The name *puppy-dog close* comes from the strategy developed by pet shop owners to sell puppies to the children of reluctant parents. For a variety of reasons, especially previous experience with dog ownership, many parents do not want to get their child a dog. They are afraid that the dog will poop, pee, shed, gnaw, bark, whine, and a variety of other things. But parents love their children.

At a certain point, the child often becomes fixated on the idea of getting a dog. The youngster then asks about getting a puppy, over and over, until the parents finally agree to go with the child to a pet store, just to "take a look."

The pet shop owner is aware of this dynamic. He shows a variety of puppies to the child. When the child falls in love with a particular puppy, and the parents are still hesitant, the pet shop owner says, "Why don't you take the puppy home for the weekend? If you don't like the puppy, you can bring him back on Monday for a full refund."

The parents, secretly hoping that the child will lose interest in the puppy by the end of the weekend, agree to take the puppy home. In many cases, they turn out to be right. The *child* loses interest in the puppy—but the parents fall in love with it. By Sunday night, they want the puppy more than the child does. The sale is made.

LET THEM TRY IT OUT

In the same way, many successful companies encourage the prospect to take the product and try it out before making a decision. Some companies today are offering a thirty-day trial ownership for a new car. They promise that if the buyer does not like the car at the end of thirty days, he can bring it back for a full refund.

When Canon photocopiers invaded the U.S. market, after the exclusive Xerox patents had expired, Canon had a simple marketing strategy. Their salespeople would visit businesses and offer to install one of their copiers for a one-month free trial. At the end of the month, if the business owner was not happy with the copier, she could simply call them and have it removed. On the other hand, if she liked the copier, they would set her up on a long-term lease, with great prices, a tremendous service contract, and all kinds of features and benefits that she was not currently receiving from the rival copier.

One company I worked with had literally hundreds of copiers out "on loan." In no time at all, they dominated the copier business in the city. Their copiers were so enjoyable to use that, once people had tried them for a month, the staff would be fighting to keep them and to get rid of whatever else they had been using.

LOWER THEIR NATURAL RESISTANCE

Prospects are skeptical about any new product or service. But at the same time, they are *creatures of habit*. If they try something and they like it, they quickly become comfortable with it. Once they have become comfortable with it, it is easier for them mentally to continue using it than it is for them to discontinue it.

When you are offering an excellent product or service, one that brings about high levels of customer satisfaction, let them try it out. When you allow prospects to sample it for any period of time, you can often make the sale easier than you might have thought.

OFFER A FREE TRIAL

We have a self-storage business with several hundred units for rent. Many people have crowded closets and cluttered garages, but they have never thought of putting their excess furniture and possessions into a self-storage unit. To counter this, we offer them one free month. They can move all their excess possessions out of their home and into their own private self-storage unit a few blocks away for thirty days. After that, if they are not satisfied, they can came and get all of their possessions and move them back home. What do you think happens?

The answer is obvious. Once people experience the convenience of cleaning out their closets, clearing out their garages, and moving all their seldom-used materials to a

When you are offering an excellent product or service, one that brings about high levels of customer satisfaction, let them try it out.

self-storage, they very seldom want to go through the time and trouble of moving all those things back home again. They quickly begin to see the self-storage unit as an extension of their own homes or apartments. It becomes like an additional room in their homes where they can store things that they hardly ever use. This is the primary reason why the self-storage business is booming everywhere. It is a perfect example of the puppy-dog close.

The Ben Franklin Close

This is one of the oldest closing techniques of all. It was first developed by the American statesman, inventor, and diplomat Ben Franklin in Philadelphia in 1765. The reason it is popular is because it is a close that exactly corresponds with the way your mind makes a major decision of any kind.

Unless you are acting emotionally and impulsively, before you make a serious decision, you think it through point by point. You consider the pros and cons of the decision, the positives and negatives. You analyze the reasons for buying and compare them against the reasons for not buying. At the end of your analysis, you weigh and balance the evidence and make your decision, yes or no.

The *Ben Franklin close* does exactly this. At the end of the sales conversation, you can say something like, "Mr. Prospect, you want to make the very best decision with regard to this product, don't you?"

"Yes, of course I do."

USE A SHEET OF PAPER

You say, "Well, let's use the method that Ben Franklin used to use when he had to make an important decision. As you know, he was one of the best decision makers of his time, the first self-made millionaire in America, and one of the most famous inventors, politicians, and scholars of the American Revolution.

"What Ben Franklin would do to make a decision is he would take a piece of paper [you do this as you are talking] and he would draw a line down the center. On one side, he would write all the reasons *in favor* of the decision, and on the other side, he would write all the reasons *opposed* to the decision."

You then take the piece of paper and write "Reasons For" at the top of one column and "Reasons Against" at the top of the other column.

Now say, "Let's look at some of the reasons this product *might* be a good choice for you." Then you write down the most attractive feature of your product or service and remind the prospect of the benefit that he would enjoy from that feature. "Do you agree?"

You then write the number 2, the second feature, and again remind the prospect of the benefit that this feature provides. Once you get his acknowledgment, go on to the third feature and benefit, and so on, until you have written down as many as ten different reasons why the prospect should buy this product or service.

"Have we covered everything?" you say.

When the prospect answers, "Yes, it looks like you've covered everything," you then give the page over to him and say, "Now, you write down any reasons that might argue against your going ahead with this idea."

The prospect may say, "Well, let me think. There is the price." He will then write down the price. Meanwhile, you wait patiently, saying nothing. Let the prospect figure out all the reasons against the offering *by himself*.

Most prospects can only think of two or three reasons not to buy a product. You then compare these reasons with the ten reasons you have given for going ahead immediately. When the prospect can no longer think of any more reasons opposed to the decision, you can say, "Well, it looks like you've made your decision."

The prospect will often look at the two lists and say, "Yes, I guess I have."

Finish with, "Why don't we get started on this right away?"

SIMPLE BUT POWERFUL

Not long ago, I ran into one of my graduates on an airplane. He is a very successful, high-earning commercial real estate agent. He told me that he had been working for six months on a complex deal involving a trade for cash, land, and commercial buildings with a large financial institution and a real estate conglomerate. He had been going back and forth on this transaction with the vice president for several weeks, but was unable to get him to come to a conclusion.

Finally, he got back together with his client and said, "Why don't we use the Ben Franklin decision-making method on this?"

He said he was surprised that the vice president agreed immediately. He pulled out a sheet of paper, drew the line down the center, and then went through the features and benefits in favor of this offering, one by one, for about half an hour. He then asked the vice president, the decision maker, to write down his opposing reasons. As expected, the vice president could only think of two or three reasons why they shouldn't go ahead with the transaction. At the end of this process, the vice president compared the two lists, looked back up at the real estate agent, and said, "Let's do it!" And the deal was sealed.

The agent told me, "Brian, I had heard about that Ben Franklin close for years, but I thought it was a bit corny, so I never tried it. But when I used it the first time, my commissions on that sale were more than I had earned in the entire previous year. It was quite amazing."

The Order-Sheet Close

This is a fast and effective way to close any transaction where an order sheet is involved. There are different variations of this close that you should memorize, especially if it is relevant to the product or service you sell.

The first variation occurs when you have spoken to the prospect, presented your product, and he fully understands what he gets and why it is of value to him. You then take out an order sheet or sales contract and start filling it in, without asking the prospect whether or not he wants to buy. "By the way, what is today's date?" you might ask as you glance at the buyer, or "What is your correct mailing address?"

If the prospect gives you today's date or his mailing address, the sale is in the bag.

YOUR POOR MEMORY

But sometimes the prospect will stop you by saying, "Wait a minute; I haven't decided to buy this yet."

You respond, "Oh, don't worry. I just have a terrible memory for details, and I like to write everything down as we go along. If you decide not to go ahead today, it will be all right. I'll just throw the order form away. OK?" You then continue writing.

Each time the prospect gives you another detail, write it on the order sheet, just as if you are trying to keep track of the sales conversation. The prospect will soon become accustomed to seeing you write down the details. Every additional detail written makes the order sheet more *personalized* for that customer. Eventually, he starts to identify with the order sheet, seeing it as an expression of his tastes and preferences.

The power of the order-sheet close is simple. The more information the prospect gives you and allows you to put in writing, the more committed he becomes to buying the product or service.

Once the order sheet is complete, look up at the prospect and say, "Now, what is the correct spelling of your last name?"

If the prospect gives you the exact spelling of his last name, "J-O-N-E-S," his decision to buy is certain. You can

WINNING CLOSING TECHNIQUES II | 153

then ask for his first name and middle initial, his correct mailing address, his zip code, and his telephone number. The sale is made.

The power of the order-sheet close is simple. The more information the prospect gives you and allows you to put in writing, the more committed he becomes to buying the product or service at the end of the conversation.

Top salespeople use this closing technique to sell hundreds of thousands of dollars' worth of their products every year. Personally, I've always been astonished at how easy it is to use. Try it for yourself and see. You will be as amazed as well.

The Negative-Answer Close

Another variation of the order-sheet close is the *negative-answer close*. First, you ask all of the pertinent questions so that you fully understand what the customer wants or needs. Then you present your product or service as the perfect solution. Finally, you ask your confirming question: "Do you have any other questions or concerns that I haven't covered?"

When the prospect says, "No, you seem to have covered everything," take out your order sheet, write today's date on the top, and begin filling out the details, without referring to the customer or asking for permission. Act exactly as if the no to your confirming question is a yes to your offering.

The Relevant-Story Close

Nobel Prize-winning research has been done into the subject of "dual-brain laterality." This is an academic way of saying that human beings have both a left and a right "brain," each having completely different functions. The left brain, for example, is used to process details in a linear fashion, one after the other.

The right brain, on the other hand, integrates information and is activated by pictures, music, and stories. All buying decisions are made by the right brain, so this is what you must appeal to.

With the *relevant-story close*, you activate the decision-making side of the customer's brain by telling a story of a customer who bought your product or service and was happy with the purchase. Whenever a prospect hears a *story* about a happy customer, she is motivated to want to be in the same situation as that happy customer, using your product and getting similar results. And this is exactly what you had in mind.

> *All buying decisions are made by the right brain, so this is what you must appeal to.*

Prospects will forget all the data, features, and fine points of your product or service within twenty-four hours, but they will remember the stories you tell about happy customers for weeks, months, and even years. Tell as many of them as possible.

TELL A HAPPY STORY

One of the best techniques that I have found is what I call a "by the way" story. "By the way," you say, "this reminds me of Susan Smith, one of our customers from XYZ Company. Just last week, she told me that she had been concerned about our high price before she bought this item, but afterward, she found that the additional benefits she got from a slightly higher price were greatly in excess of the difference in cost."

Whenever you use a relevant-story close, talk about how satisfied people are now that they are using what you are selling. Since the deepest human motivation is the desire to be happy, when you tell about other happy customers, you trigger an unconscious desire on the part of your prospect to become a happy customer as well.

TELL A SAD STORY

A friend of mine, one of the top insurance agents in the country, uses this relevant-story close very effectively. When the prospect seems to be resistant to purchasing life insurance, he takes out the copy of a document describing what happened to a successful businessman who died with a net worth of $1.5 million.

Unfortunately, this businessman was underinsured. By the time taxes were paid on his estate and all debts were settled, his company had to be sold at a bargain-basement price. Within two years, the small amount of money left over was gone, and his widow was destitute. She was forced to move in with her grown children as a permanent house-guest. She didn't even have social security.

Once a prospect had heard that story, he became very interested in finding out what he could do to make sure the same thing did not happen to him and his wife. From then on, the sale was easy.

HEROES AND VILLAINS

There is one other kind of relevant story that you can use. This is the story of someone who decided *not* to buy your product, or even worse, bought a similar product from a competitor at a lower price. You tell what happened to that buyer and how unhappy he was with the results of his purchase. Make sure to add that this customer, whom you spoke to just recently, really regrets not buying from you. This kind of a negative story can often trigger a positive buying decision.

HAVE SEVERAL STORIES

Relevant stories should be part of your sales repertoire. Just as a comedian memorizes a series of humorous stories and anecdotes, you as a professional salesperson should memorize a series of relevant stories that you can drop into your sales conversation and use to counter objections and sales resistance at the end of your presentation. One relevant story can turn a neutral or indifferent prospect into an enthusiastic buyer of your product or service.

The Walk-Away Close

One of the most common responses you will hear in selling anything is, "Let me think about it" or any variation thereof.

You can often save the sale by using a *walk-away close*. Like this:

Let's say the prospect says, "Well, I'd like to shop around and see what else is available before I make a decision." You respond by saying, "Mr. Prospect, that's a good idea. But here's the fact: We have been doing business here for many years. Most of our customers are repeat customers who come from referrals from other repeat customers. Every one of them has shopped all over town before they finally came back here and bought from us. You can go out and check other prices, but why put yourself through all that trouble? You're probably going to end up back here anyway. Why don't you make the decision right now? We can wrap it up for you and load it in your car, or we can have it out to you tomorrow morning."

Offer to Relieve the Stress

What we have found is that a buying decision *unmade* remains a problem *unsolved* in a customer's mind. It is a source of tension, and often distraction. When you help a customer make a buying decision *now*, you solve his problem, relieve his tension, and free him to get on with other things.

In follow-up interviews with customers, researchers have found that once they decide to buy something, it drops off their mental radar screens and they begin thinking about other parts of their life and work. The decision loses its importance as soon as it is made.

When you use this walk-away close, by encouraging them to make the buying decision now rather than walking away, you are offering to save the prospect all the time and energy that he would have to expend to talk with other suppliers and get additional prices.

Remember, *logic does make sales.* If you give him a logical reason for buying from you immediately, you can often stop him from walking away.

THE TODAY-ONLY CLOSE

If the prospect insists and says, "Well, I still really think I should go and check, because I want to be sure that I'm getting the best deal," you can use a variation of the walk-away close called the *today-only close.*

You say, "Mrs. Prospect, I'll tell you what. This is the end of our fiscal period, and if you will just take it today, I will be able to give you a special, extra discount on this item."

There is a rule in selling: no urgency, no sale.

To get the prospect to buy immediately, you often have to give her a reason, an incentive, for going ahead now. You can say that this is your last item or that you are going to have a price increase starting tomorrow, or that this is the last day of a sales contest, and if she buys it today, you will get a special bonus. This is *why* you can give her an additional incentive for buying now.

This type of close carries one caveat: an added incentive, or a "kicker," is only an inducement to buy if you present it *at the very end* of the sales conversation. If you offer a special bonus of any kind *before* that, it will have little or no impact on the prospect's buying decision. He will include your incentive as part of the offering, and you will have to offer even more to get the sale. Save it until the last moment.

EXTRACT A PROMISE

The third variation of the walk-away close is what you use when the prospect is absolutely determined to go and check other products and prices before he makes a decision. In this case you very graciously concede, and instead of arguing, you actually encourage him to go.

"Mr. Prospect, I understand exactly how you feel. It's a good idea that you go and check prices at other places. But I want you to *promise* me one thing. Before you make a final decision, come back and talk to me, and I'll give you the best deal in town."

By saying this, you are planting a seed of doubt in the prospect's mind. By promising to give him the best deal in town, at the end of his shopping trip, you are almost forcing him to come back and see you before he makes an absolute decision.

Refuse to Show Your Cards

Sometimes he will say, "Well, what is the very best deal that you can give me?"

You answer, "Mr. Prospect, I know that you are going to go and look around. By all means, please do so. But when you have checked out our competitors, and *only then*, come back to me. I'll give you the best deal in town."

The prospect must now go and trudge from place to place, demanding to know the very best price that he can get from each seller, and finally, bring them all back to you to find out the "best deal in town."

Two Ways to Close the Sale

When the prospect finally comes back and shows you the best deals that he can get anywhere else, this is how you close the sale. First, if you can beat the others on price, then simply offer a price that is a few dollars less than the best price he has been able to find. Once you have given it, take out your order sheet, ask for the correct spelling of his last name, and begin filling it out. If it happens that you cannot beat a competitor on the basis of price, deflect the customer's attention away from price and onto the quality, service, delivery, warranties, and follow-up support that your company can offer. Say, "Mr. Prospect, the best deal for you is not simply the lowest price. It is a combination of several factors. Here is what we include in our price, which, all things considered, makes this a better deal for you than anyone else can give you."

ASK FOR THE SALE

You then use a summary close or a Ben Franklin close to repeat the benefits that the prospect gets and why these are more important to him than simply a lower price. You point out, "This price might be a little higher than one of our competitors', but it is a much better deal for you, all things considered."

By this time, the prospect is tired of going around and looking for the best price. He has a problem unsolved, and you are offering a solution. If you give him a logical reason for buying now, he will more than likely go ahead. All that is required from you is a closing question: "Why don't you take it?"

The Lost-Sale Close

Every now and then, when a prospect asks you to leave your sales material with him so he can think about it, there is nothing you can do to get him to budge. He has a hidden objection, and he won't tell you what it is. In this case, instead of arguing or insisting, you gracefully concede and prepare to leave. Say, "Mr. Prospect, thank you very much for your time. I know how busy you are. I'll get back to you a little bit later, and perhaps we can talk about this some more."

GET HIM TO RELAX

When you say this, the prospect will always agree. The pressure is off. He is happy that the sales discussion is over and that you are leaving. He is already beginning to think about what he is going to do when you are out of sight.

As he contemplates your departure and his getting back to work, his sales resistance drops, and he relaxes. Like a boxer when the bell rings at the end of the round, he drops his hands and his guard.

Close your briefcase, stand up, shake hands with the prospect, thank him again for his time, and turn to go. But as you reach the door and put your hand on the knob, turn around and say these words: "Mr. Prospect, just before I go, may I ask you one question?"

When he agrees, say, "Mr. Prospect, I've tried to present my product information the very best way I know how, and I feel like I've somehow done something wrong. I'd really appreciate it if you'd just tell me this: What was the real reason you didn't buy today?"

The prospect, who is now relaxed and happy, contemplating what he will do when you leave, may then say, "Well, now that you ask, the real reason I didn't buy was this . . ."

Now You Know

Whatever reason he gives you, this is the *final objection*, or key reason, that is holding him back from buying. Once you know it, you have an opportunity to answer that objection to his satisfaction and make the sale.

You say, "Mr. Prospect, thank you. That's my fault. I obviously didn't explain that to you properly. Let me show you what we can do to handle that for you."

You take your hand off the doorknob, walk right back, sit down, and say, "This will take just one more second," and you start closing on that final objection.

For example, if he says, "Well, the reason I didn't buy today was because I'm not really convinced that your machine will produce the number of copies I require," you say, "Mr. Prospect, you mean I didn't explain that properly? Well, we have a warranty that covers exactly that issue. If we could give you a written guarantee of satisfaction, would you be prepared to go ahead right now?"

Once you have the final objection, answer it and ask for the order once more. Only now, there is no more sales resistance. The customer is completely relaxed and will often buy if you give him one more reason.

FLYING HIGH

At my sales seminar in Charlotte recently, a young man came up to me and said, "Mr. Tracy, I just closed the biggest sale of my career. I made a $2,000 commission from a sale that I knew I had lost before I used your lost-sale close."

He went on to tell me, "I had made my presentation, and the prospect would not give me an answer. As I got up to go and I put my hand on the doorknob, I remembered the words from your program. I turned to him and asked him, 'Mr. Prospect, please help me out. What was the real reason you decided not to buy today?' And he told me! I turned around, sat back down, opened my briefcase, and answered his last objection. And he decided to buy. I earned two grand from a sale that I had lost just two minutes before by using that closing technique."

Closing on Referrals

One of the fastest ways to increase your income, with less time and effort, is to develop a series of ways to get referrals from both prospects and satisfied customers. A

....

A referral is worth ten to fifteen times a cold call.

....

referral is worth ten to fifteen times a cold call. This means that it takes one-tenth to one-fifteenth the time and energy to close a sale with a referral than it takes to start cold-calling and finding brand-new prospects.

The key issue in selling is *credibility*. When you get a referral, you piggyback on the credibility of the person referring you. Instead of having to build your credibility from the ground up, you walk in with the credibility of the person who recommended you.

BE REFERABLE

The key to getting referrals is *being referable*. The major objection to giving referrals is that the customer is not convinced that you will take good care of his friend or colleague. When you treat your customers well and give them excellent quality and service, they will feel more comfortable recommending you to other people that they know. When you are polite, punctual, professional, and prepared every time, people will want to share you with others.

ASK EVERYONE

Get referrals by *asking for them* on every occasion, after every sales call and after every sale.

You can even ask for referrals *in advance* of selling. You can say, "Ms. Prospect, I am going to show you something that I think you will really like. But whether or not this is the right thing for you at this time, if you like what I show you, would you give me the names of two or three other people who may like it as well?"

When you ask for referrals in this way, in advance of selling, you set the stage. If your product or service is attractive and well presented, the prospect will feel obligated to give you the names of two or three other people at the end of your presentation, whether she buys or not. The key is for you to ask.

MOVE FAST ON REFERRALS

When you get a referral, follow up on it immediately. After you have spoken to the referral, report back to the source of the referral. Call the person who gave you the name and tell her what happened. Always speak in a complimentary way about the referral, whether she bought or not.

When you report back to the source of a referral, always wrap up your conversation by saying, "By the way, would you happen to know two or three *other* nice people like this person I could also talk to?"

SEND A GIFT

If the referral turns into a sale, think about sending a gift to the source of the referral. If you earn a substantial commission on a referral sale, send a high-quality fruit basket with a personal note thanking her for that referral.

Call back a couple of days later to ensure that the basket was delivered. The person you call will always be delighted at having received the fruit basket. She will thank you profusely. Take this opportunity to ask if she knows any other "nice people" on whom you could call.

SEND THANK-YOU NOTES

Finally, send thank-you notes to each person who gives you a referral. Then send thank-you notes to the people to whom they refer you. Send thank-yous on every occasion, and always include your business card. The more thank-you notes you send out, the better the reputation you build in the market and the more referable you become.

Many sales professionals I know find that within a few months of implementing a referral strategy, they no longer have time to prospect. They have so many referrals to call on that they are busy all day long following up on them.

When you begin taking these referral-building steps, you will find yourself developing a steady stream of referrals from all directions.

DEVELOP YOUR OWN STRATEGIES

A good friend of mine, one of the highest-paid people in his industry, has an interesting strategy for getting referrals. In December of each year, he phones and then visits all his clients from the past year, and often from years before. He makes it clear that the purpose of his call is to be sure that they are perfectly happy with the services his company has provided to them.

He meets with customers, asks a lot of questions, takes notes, and promises to follow up on any difficulties that they are having. He then asks them for referrals for the months ahead. With this strategy, he starts every year with more than one hundred prospects to call on.

ASK THE RIGHT QUESTIONS

Use the right words when you ask for feedback. If you ask a customer, "How is everything going?" he will always say, "Fine." But here's the rule: if a customer is not complaining, it usually means that he is not happy for some reason. The reason he says, "Fine," is because he doesn't want to get into an argument with you.

> *If a customer is not complaining, it usually means that he is not happy for some reason. The reason he says, "Fine," is because he doesn't want to get into an argument with you.*

When you make a service call on a customer, instead of asking, "How's it going?" you ask, "Is there anything that we can do to *improve our services* to you in the future?" Whenever you refer a customer to the future, to an ideal future state, he will almost invariably tell you the specific things you can do to make his experience with you and his company even better next time. This is what you want to hear, more than anything else. Then, when you get these ideas, promise to follow up on them right away.

"OTHER NICE PEOPLE LIKE YOU"

The last thing you do, after any customer service visit, is to ask the "other nice people like you" question that we've already covered: "By the way, I really like working with people like you. Would you happen to know any other nice people like you that I could talk to about my services?" After you have asked for *his* input and promised to take care of *his* problems, he will be open to giving you the names of other people he knows who may be interested in what you have to offer. Write down the names and phone numbers. Ask him if he would help you out by giving these people a call and telling them that you will be contacting them. By and large, your customers will be pleased to help.

THE ALTERNATIVE CLOSE ON REFERRALS

Here is a simple process you can use to implement these recommendations. Ask the prospect, "Bill, would you happen to know the names of *two or three* other nice people like yourself that I could speak to?" (the alternative close).

The prospect will almost invariably choose *two* rather than three. Take out your pen and poise it over your pad, ready to write (the suggestive close). He will shuffle through his Rolodex, PalmPilot, or BlackBerry and give you two names and phone numbers. Once you have recorded these on your pad, you then ask, "Bill, which of these two should I phone first?" Bill will tell you which one.

Now say, "Bill, you know this person better than I do. Would *you* call him up and tell him that I will be calling for an appointment, say, next Thursday afternoon?"

PEOPLE WILL HELP YOU IF YOU ASK

Bill knows exactly what you are asking and will usually help you out. He will call the person and probably get straight through. He will then tell that person that he is speaking to you and that you will be calling him. While he is on the phone, take this opportunity to mouth a suggestion to him: "Three o'clock next Thursday?" and Bill will almost always ask the person on the phone if that time will work for him or her.

By the time Bill gets off the phone, he will have set up an appointment for you with a qualified referral.

Now that Bill has called one person, calling one more person is no problem for him. Ask him to, and he will call the second person and set up that appointment for you as well. You will often leave his office with two locked-in referrals, built on the credibility of the person you just spoke to.

RESOLVE TO SELL "BY REFERRAL ONLY"

The highest-paid salespeople work on the basis of referrals only. They make it a regular part of their sales work to ask for referrals from everyone, everywhere they go. They have developed so many different contacts and sources of referrals that they no longer have time to prospect for new business.

When you visit a referral from a happy customer, the sale is 90 percent made before you even open your mouth. This is the fastest and most predictable way for you to move into the top ranks of the highest money earners in your field. And the key? Just ask.

Action Exercises:

1. Select one closing technique each week and read it over and over until you memorize the words; practice it aloud repeatedly.

2. Identify the most common price objections you hear and develop ways to overcome them.

3. Make a decision today to work by referral only; ask each customer and noncustomer for the names of prospects you can talk to.

4. Plan and rehearse several different ways to close the sale in the course of your presentation; the more you ask for the order, the likelier you will get it.

5. Develop and rehearse a series of glad as well as sad stories that you can use in your sales conversation to reduce resistance and close the sale; stories are powerful.

6. Be referable; do everything you can to be such a professional salesperson that everyone you talk to will want to recommend you to their friends and colleagues.

7. Ask for the order; as soon as you answer the remaining objection, take the initiative and immediately move into closing the sale; this is where you "putt for dough."

Work joyfully and peacefully, knowing that the right thoughts and the right efforts will inevitably bring about right results.

—James Allen

6

DOUBLE YOUR PRODUCTIVITY, DOUBLE YOUR INCOME

*He who every morning plans the transactions of the day
and follows out that plan, carries a thread that will
guide him through the labyrinth of the most busy life.*

—Victor Hugo

YOUR ABILITY TO MANAGE YOUR TIME CAN BE THE CRITI-
cal factor in your success as a sales professional. The quality of your time management often determines the quality
of your life.

When I first began selling, I saw time management as one
of many subjects that I considered in the course of my sales
career. I saw it as a planet that orbited around the sun of my
life. It was only when I realized that time management *is* the

sun of my life, and that everything else going on is merely planets that orbit it, that I began to double and triple my efficiency. You can do the same.

How You Think About Time

How you think about your income largely determines the amount of money you earn and how much you accomplish. Average salespeople think about their income in terms of how much they make each month and each year. But top salespeople think about their income in terms of their *hourly rate*, and they are determined to make every hour pay for itself.

Top salespeople think about their income in terms of their hourly rate, and they are determined to make every hour pay for itself.

When you think of your income in terms of a month or a year, it is very easy for you to waste time day by day. According to a study at Columbia University, the average salesperson only works ninety minutes per day. His first sales call is not made until about 11:00 AM, and his last sales call is made at about 3:00 in the afternoon. In between, he is warming up, hanging out at the vending machines, chatting idly, or engaging in other time-wasting activities.

Determine Your Hourly Rate

Top salespeople, however, think in terms of how much they want to earn by dividing their annual income goal by

2,000, the number of hours in a sales year, and then committing themselves to earning that amount *each hour*.

For example, if you want to earn $50,000 a year, divided by 2,000, your income goal is $25 per hour. If you want to double your income to $100,000 per year, you must earn $50 per hour, *every single* hour. You cannot reach your desired income goal if you do not do the things that pay you that kind of income.

> *Salespeople only get paid for results. As they say in hunting, "You can only eat what you kill."*

When you work for a fixed salary, you get paid the same amount as long as you show up at your place of work. But salespeople are different. Salespeople only get paid for results. As they say in hunting, "You can only eat what you kill."

The Law of Three

In our Advanced Coaching Programs for successful entrepreneurs and sales professionals, we teach the *law of three*. This law says that, no matter how many things you do in a week or a month, there are only *three activities* that pay you your desired hourly rate. These three activities account for more than 90 percent of your income. The secret to sales success, or success in any field, is this: *do more and more of fewer things, but more important things, and get better and better at each of them.*

In selling, no matter what the product, the only three activities that will pay your desired hourly rate are *prospecting, presenting,* and *closing.* Only when you are engaged in these three core activities are you actually working.

You Wake Up Unemployed

Salespeople wake up unemployed each morning and remain unemployed until they get face-to-face with someone who can and will buy within a reasonable period of time. Only then does the workday begin.

When we say that the average salesperson *works* ninety minutes per day, this is because the average salesperson only spends ninety minutes each day prospecting, presenting, and closing.

INCREASE YOUR FACE TIME

Another way that you can determine if you are working or not is by measuring the amount of "face time" you spend with qualified prospects each day. Your job is to get face-to-face with people who can buy, and then to sell your products or services to them. Driving to a prospect's home or place of business, rearranging your sales materials, writing up your sales reports, and listening to music in your car may take place during the sales day, but these are not core activities. They pay nothing.

One of the simplest ways for you to double your income is to double the amount of time you spend prospecting, presenting, and closing, i.e., double the number of minutes you spend face-to-face with qualified prospects. Every hour of every day you should be asking yourself, *would I pay someone else $25 or $50 per hour to do what I am doing, right now?*

If you would not pay someone else your desired hourly rate to do what you are doing at any given time, stop doing it immediately and start prospecting, presenting, and closing. As Zig Ziglar says, "If you will be hard on yourself, life will be easy on you. But if you insist on being easy on yourself, life is going to be very hard on you."

The Keys to Time Management

Since they are only working when they are *face-to-face* with a real, live prospect or customer, top salespeople do their preparation and organization work on nonselling time. They plan their weeks each weekend. They plan each day the night before. They plan and organize their sales work before the selling day and in the evenings. But during the times that customers are available, they concentrate single-mindedly on spending more time face-to-face with those customers. This is where the rubber meets the road.

Eliminate the Time Wasters in Selling

TIME WASTER #1: PROCRASTINATION AND DELAY

The first major time waster in selling is procrastination and delay. This occurs when you find every conceivable reason to put off getting out there with people who can and will buy from you.

Everyone procrastinates. There is always too much to do and too little time. The difference between successes and failures is determined by their choices about what they put off. *Losers* put off the important things that could make a significant difference in their lives. *Winners* put off low-value tasks and activities, those things that make very little difference whether they are done or not.

Stop wasting time. According to Robert Half International, half of all working time, in all fields, is wasted. Most of this wasted time is taken up with coffee breaks, phone calls, personal business, shopping, or other useless activities that make no contribution to your work. When people do work, the average person works about thirty-two hours per week. Of this, sixteen hours are wasted and only sixteen hours are spent doing the job. Of these sixteen *working* hours, many of them are spent on things that are fun and easy, rather than hard and necessary.

Resolve to overcome procrastination. The best way to overcome procrastination is to plan each day in advance, set priorities on your activities, and then make your first sales call as early as you possibly can. Get up and get going. When you launch quickly into a workday, doing something important as early as possible, you will work at a higher level of effectiveness all day long.

When you find yourself procrastinating, say to yourself, *do it now! Do it now! Do it now!* These words motivate you to get started. When you repeat them often enough, you drive this message deep into your subconscious mind, where it serves as a trigger to get you going and keep you moving throughout the day.

People are major time wasters. To eliminate delays, play your own game. Work your own schedule. Don't associate with people who have time to associate with *you*. People are among the biggest time wasters in the world of work. Stay away from other folks who procrastinate. They will only drag you down.

There is nothing wrong with drinking coffee, but do it on the go, or with your prospects and customers. There is nothing wrong with stopping for lunch, but eat it quickly. Don't make an afternoon ritual out of lunch. Whenever possible, have lunch on the way to see customers or have it *with* customers and prospects. Forget lunching with coworkers. This is a waste of time and keeps you away from your primary sales activities.

> *In selling, no matter what the product, the only three activities that will pay your desired hourly rate are prospecting, presenting, and closing. Only when you are engaged in these three core activities are you actually working.*

TIME WASTER #2: THE INCOMPLETE SALES CALL

Another major time waster is the incomplete sales call, requiring a *callback*. This occurs when you have not thoroughly prepared your presentation or taken all the materials you need for your sales call. When you are with the customer, you find that you are missing the correct order forms, prices, or materials that you need to close the sale. You then have to make arrangements to go back and see the prospect a second time, something that often does not happen.

Poor sales skills. Incompletion of the sales call can often be caused by poor sales skills. You do not know how to answer objections or to close the sale. When you arrive at that point in the sales presentation, you don't know what to say or how to deal with it. You inadvertently activate the prospect's response: "Let me think it over."

As I wrote about in the introduction, when I started off selling in my early twenties, the only job I could get was straight-commission selling, cold-calling from office to office, selling $20 memberships in a restaurant club. With the discount card, the customer could get 10 to 20 percent discounts in about one hundred different restaurants around the city. It would pay for itself with one usage. It should have been an easy sell. But it wasn't.

Forget lunching with coworkers. This is a waste of time and keeps you away from your primary sales activities.

Because I didn't know how to sell, I would cold call, make my presentation, and at the end of the sale, I wouldn't know what to say. The prospect would say, "Well, leave it with me, and let me think it over."

I would thank her very much, make a note to call back on her in a couple of days, and go on with my work. Invariably, when I called back, the prospect was not in, was in a meeting, was not available, was not interested, or had forgotten what I had spoken to her about in the first place. It was very frustrating.

CHANGE YOUR APPROACH

One day I had a revelation: the reason I was only making two or three sales a week was because I was continually offering to call back after the prospect had had a chance to think about it. I decided, from that moment on, that I would not call back anymore. I would ask for the order, yes or no, after every presentation.

For me, this took a lot of courage. The very next person I called on, at the end of my presentation, said, "Well, it looks pretty good; let me think about it. Call me back next week."

I took a deep breath and replied, "I'm sorry, but I don't make callbacks."

The prospect looked straight at me and said, "What did you say?"

I replied, "I'm sorry, I don't make callbacks. Mr. Prospect, this is not a big decision. It is an excellent product. It pays for itself in one usage. Everything you need to know to make a buying decision, you already know. Why don't you just take it?"

And the prospect replied, "All right, I'll take it."

A MAJOR TURNING POINT

When I walked out of that meeting, I was a new salesman. From then on I didn't make callbacks. My whole sales life changed. I walked into the next office, got the same response

("Let me think it over"), and gave the same reply ("I don't make callbacks"). The second person I spoke to bought as well.

The fact is that people do not think it over. Instead, they will forget you ever lived by the time you get out of the building.

Then the third, and the fourth, and the fifth. In that one day, I sold more than I was accustomed to selling in an entire week.

The fact is that people do not think it over. Instead, they will forget you ever lived by the time you get out of the building.

When you call back, they will have no idea what you are talking about or why they might have been interested in the first place.

SHARPEN YOUR SKILLS

Over the years I have learned that a primary reason for time wastage in selling is that salespeople simply do not know how to sell. They do not identify needs clearly. They do not present properly. They do not know how to answer objections intelligently. And they don't know how to close professionally. As a result, they go from customer to customer but make few sales. All this can be overcome by improving your sales skills and increasing your level of determination.

TIME WASTER #3: INACCURACIES AND DEFICIENCIES

You waste a lot of time in selling when you find yourself with a prospect, but without all the information needed to make an intelligent presentation. You may have the wrong facts, the wrong figures, or the wrong specifications. You may present the wrong price for the wrong order for the wrong materials. You may have misunderstood what the prospect said she wanted and made a proposal that does not solve the prospect's problem or satisfy her need.

SMALL MISTAKES CAUSE BIG PROBLEMS

Some years ago, in presenting a building for sale to a commercial purchaser, I put together a proposal on the building with a breakdown of revenues, expenses, and expected rates of return. I had it typed by my assistant, but I did not take the time to review it carefully. As a result, I was off by one decimal point. Instead of a 15 percent net cash flow on investment, the proposal showed a building that yielded 1.5 percent, only one-tenth of the potential.

The prospect was very sharp. He quickly reviewed the proposal, checked the numbers, and then chucked the proposal back at me across the desk. "Why are you wasting my time with something like this?"

The numbers were wrong, and it cost me the deal. My credibility was shot. The prospect would not meet with me again. From that day forward, I have checked every number in every proposal before it went out.

You should also be sure that all of your paperwork is done correctly, and check it in advance before you go to see the prospect. Never assume that everything will be all right. As time management expert Alex McKenzie said, "Errant assumptions lie at the root of every failure."

TIME WASTER #4: LACK OF PRODUCT KNOWLEDGE

This weakness can cost you hours of hard work. It boils down to ignorance of the product or service you are selling. This is invariably caused by laziness on the part of the salesperson. Fortunately, it can be very easily overcome with time and study.

You should be intimately familiar with everything that your product or service can do. Know what your competitors offer that is different from your product or service. Be clear why and how your product or service is superior to anything else on the market.

BE ABLE TO ANSWER ANY QUESTION

When the prospect asks, "If I have this problem or need, will your product or service do this or that for me?" you should be able to answer clearly and correctly.

If you aren't sure of the answer and you start to mumble and stumble, you look foolish. The prospect instantly senses that you do not know what you are talking about. Your credibility goes down the drain. The prospect's interest in dealing with you vanishes. You are soon back out on the street, wondering what happened.

Good product knowledge is the foundation of all sales success. The very best salespeople I have met have memorized their product's specifications. If they lost all their brochures and sales information, they could still give a compelling sales presentation with just the information stored in their own heads. It should be the same with you.

TIME WASTER #5: POOR PREPARATION

Thorough preparation separates the sheep from the goats among professional salespeople. The top salesperson takes the time to diligently study every detail of her product or service. She reviews and then reviews again. She takes notes. She decides in advance that no one will ever ask her a question that she cannot answer intelligently and completely.

The very best salespeople memorize their product's specifications. If they lost all their brochures and sales information, they could still give a compelling sales presentation with just the information stored in their own heads.

One of the great benefits of thorough preparation is the *confidence* that it gives you. When you are thoroughly prepared, you are calmer, more relaxed, and more positive. You feel good about yourself. You have a positive mental attitude. As a result, you make a positive impression on the prospect and cause him or her to relax as well. The entire sales process is smoother and easier. Preparation really pays off.

TIME WASTER #6: UNCONFIRMED APPOINTMENTS

Here's a common scenario. A salesperson sets off across town to see a prospect for an appointment. It was arranged in advance, so everything should go as planned, right? But when the salesperson arrives, the prospect has been called out of town, is in a meeting, or cannot see him for some reason. As a result, he has wasted the entire trip, including the time it now takes him to get back to his office. Sometimes a salesperson can lose half a day because he did not reconfirm an appointment.

Why don't salespeople bother to reconfirm appointments? Easy. They are afraid that if they call to reconfirm, the prospect will *cancel* the appointment. They are willing to take a chance rather than to risk the rejection that they might experience.

TWO WAYS TO RECONFIRM APPOINTMENTS

There are two ways that you can reconfirm an appointment without the risk of having it canceled. First, call the prospect directly and ask (even though you already know), "Excuse me, Mr. Prospect, is our meeting tomorrow afternoon at 2:00 or 2:30?"

When the prospect says, "Oh, we're scheduled to meet at 2:00 PM," you say, "That's exactly what I thought; I'll be there at 2:00 PM sharp. I'm looking forward to seeing you."

Another way to reconfirm an appointment without losing it is to call the receptionist and ask, "Is Mr. Brown available? When the receptionist confirms that he is in the office and available, you then say, "Please tell him that this is John Jones calling, and that I will be there for my appointment with him at 10:00 AM sharp. Thank you very much."

The advantage of calling up and confirming is that it makes you look and sound more professional. It reminds the prospect of your visit and arouses a certain amount of curiosity and anticipation. It reminds the prospect to clear his calendar and make time for you.

RESCHEDULE IMMEDIATELY

Sometimes when you call to reconfirm an appointment, the prospect's assistant will say, "I'm glad you called. Mrs. Prospect has had an emergency and won't be able to meet with you today."

You immediately respond by saying, "I'm sorry to hear that, but thank you for letting me know. Perhaps we could set up a new time that would be more convenient. Do you have her calendar handy?"

USE E-MAIL TO RECONFIRM

With e-mail, you have a wonderful way to reconfirm appointments without any danger of them being canceled, at least not immediately. When you first set the appointment, get the person's e-mail address. Then, the evening before the appointment, send him an e-mail confirming that you will be there at the time agreed upon. Since the first thing people do in the morning is check their e-mail, you will have reminded him of the appointment, and he will be expecting your visit.

Many salespeople also call after hours and leave a voice mail reminding the prospect of the appointment. This is another safe and effective way to confirm.

TIME WASTER #7: POOR GEOGRAPHICAL PLANNING OF CALLS

This is a major time waster, often caused by the tendency of salespeople to *unconsciously* avoid the potential rejection that goes with selling by spreading their calls widely over a geographic area. They will make one call in the far north of the city and then set their next call in the far south of the city, spending an hour or so traveling in between. As they drive along listening to the radio, they convince themselves that because they are in motion, they are somehow at work.

You can sometimes streamline your sales business and increase your income immediately by clustering your calls geographically. Reduce the amount of traveling time between customers and you automatically increase the amount of face time that you spend with people who can buy.

Divide your sales territory into *quadrants*. Resolve to work in one quadrant each day or half day. Cluster all your calls in that quadrant for that time period. If someone in the southwest wants to see you when you are committed to working in the northeast part of the city, move him to the day that you will be in his area.

A GREAT SUCCESS STORY

After I had taught this simple process at a sales seminar, a very successful saleswoman came up to me and told me an interesting story. A couple of years earlier, she had decided to get into sales as a last resort. She had no sales experience, but she needed to support herself. She tried for six months to get a sales job with a national company, without success. Finally one of their salespeople quit, so they decided to give her a chance. Within six months, she was the top saleswoman in the country for them. They were amazed.

She said that her secret was simple. She divided her territory into four parts and then disciplined herself to work intensely in one of those four parts each day, four days per week. She disciplined herself not to travel between geographic areas. As a result, she spent more time with prospects, and got better and better at selling. The better she became, the more sales she made and the more referrals she got in the areas where she was concentrating. She eventually became one of the highest-paid professionals in her field in the nation.

TIME WASTER #8: NEEDLESS PERFECTIONISM

There is an old proverb that says, "The perfect is the enemy of the good." Salespeople who are nervous about calling on new people oftentimes insist upon having everything perfectly in order before they make the first call. They use the need for more preparation as an excuse to avoid selling. They say they must memorize every single detail.

> *The basic rule is for you to get it 80 percent right and then launch. Become good enough and knowledgeable enough on your product to start, and then get out in front of people.*

They feel compelled to check and learn every line on every form. They study their sales materials exhaustively.

This is often called *needless perfectionism*. The basic rule in this area is for you to get it 80 percent right and then launch. Become good enough and knowledgeable enough on your product to start, and then get out in front of people. As Benjamin Tregoe once said, "The very worst use of time is to do very well what need not be done at all."

You will find that the more time you spend in front of customers, the more you will learn about your product and how to sell it. There is nothing that replaces face-to-face contact and direct question-and-answer sessions with prospects.

GET UP AND GET GOING

The insistence upon getting everything perfect before you make calls can be fatal to your success. Learn what you *need* to learn; get the basics down pat. But then get up and get out there with people who can buy. Everything else will take care of itself.

The fear of rejection is like a goblin that lurks deep in your subconscious mind. When you have this fear, as everyone does to some extent, it manifests itself in your creating every conceivable excuse to avoid calling on new prospects, reconfirming appointments, and meeting those people *in person*. Remember, overcome fear by doing the thing you fear. You eliminate the fear of rejection by simply facing rejection so many times that fear is not a factor for you.

TIME WASTER #9: DISTRACTION AND MIND WANDERING

Many sales have been lost because the salesperson did not pay attention to what the prospect was saying. Perhaps the salesperson was thinking of problems at home or his plans for the weekend. Perhaps he was pondering his financial situation or his relationship with his girlfriend.

In any case, when you don't listen attentively to the prospect, you miss the nuances of what the prospect says, those subtle things that he is trying to get across. You fail to notice the looks that the prospect gives you at certain parts of your presentation that would tell you what interests him the most about your product.

Disciplines Are Learnable

Your ability to focus and concentrate keenly on the prospect and what he is saying is a *discipline*, and all disciplines can be learned. Concentration is not easy at the beginning, but it becomes easier and easier over time. (Everything is hard before it is easy.)

Sometimes you can increase your focus and your level of attention by taking careful notes while the prospect is speaking. When you practice listening techniques that include leaning forward, pausing, and questioning for clarification, this keeps you more alert to what the prospect is saying and, more important, to what he *means* by what he is saying.

Time Waster #10: Overworked and Overtired

Fatigue is a major time waster. But selling is hard work. It tires you out. It drains your energy. It burns up all your reserves. The harder you work and the more intensely you interact with people, the more fatigued you will be at the end of the day.

When you come right down to it, the energy and sparkle of your personality is the most important factor that you bring to the sales process. People do not buy products; they buy people. People don't buy what you sell, they buy *you*— and *then* they buy what you sell. When you are full of vitality and enthusiasm, you make a positive impact on the person you are talking to. When you are at your very best, you make the most sales. When you're not, you don't.

GET LOTS OF SLEEP

Most adults suffer from mild forms of sleep deprivation. They are not getting enough sleep each weeknight to perform at their best during the weekdays. Don't let this happen to you. Get to bed before ten at least five nights per week.

Many of my students have taken this advice to heart. They have increased their sleep from six or seven hours to eight hours per night, and they are absolutely amazed at the difference. They feel as if they have awakened from a drugged sleep. They did not realize that they were going through each day in a fog, not as sharp and on the ball as they could be.

TAKE CARE OF YOUR HEALTH

The chances of your making a sale are ever so enhanced if you are bright and energetic in a sales conversation. The highest-performing salespeople I know are fastidious about their health and energy. They eat the right foods, get lots of rest, and exercise vigorously. Many of the top-paid salespeople in America are marathon and even triathlon runners.

Get a good book on diet and follow it closely. Eat more fruits and vegetables. Choose high-protein breakfasts, avoiding toast, bacon, sausage, and other heavy, fatty foods. Have a salad with fish or chicken for lunch. Drink plenty of water throughout the day. Keep yourself performing at high levels by feeding yourself well so that you feel healthy and hearty throughout the day.

Imagine that you have become very wealthy in sales. You have fulfilled your lifelong dream. You bought an expensive racehorse, one that cost $500,000. If you owned an expensive racehorse, what kind of foods would you feed it? If you had invested all that money in a horse, would you feed it junk food, potato chips, soda, donuts, bagels, candy bars, and jugs of coffee? Of course not!

How much more valuable are you than a racehorse? Just as you would feed an expensive racehorse with the most nutritious foods you could possibly find, you must feed yourself with the very best foods as well. Treat yourself like the most expensive and most important person in the whole world, because you are.

How much more valuable are you than a racehorse? Just as you would feed an expensive racehorse with the most nutritious foods you could possibly find, you must feed yourself with the very best foods as well.

BECOME A HIGH-ENERGY PROFESSIONAL

Here's another old adage: "It's not the size of the dog in the fight; it's the size of the fight in the dog." It is not enough to just be physically present with a prospect. What will have the greatest impact on the sale is the amount of passion and vitality you exhibit when you are face-to-face with that person.

Resolve today to take wonderful care of your physical health. The more energy you have, the faster you will bounce back from rejection and failure. Your levels of self-confidence and self-esteem will be astronomical. You will make a positive impression on everyone you meet.

When you are tired, it's much harder for you to absorb the rejection and disappointment of daily life. They depress you and tire you out even more. But when you are fresh and well rested, you spring back from every difficulty, and you sell like a steam engine all day long.

TIME WASTER #11: LACK OF AMBITION

Perhaps the most important single quality that leads to high performance and sales success is *ambition*. To be ambitious, you must be *hungry*. You must have an intense, burning desire for sales success and the money that goes with it. You must get up each morning thinking, *I can hardly wait to get out there!*

Sales success comes from being eager to call on new prospects. When you see that by succeeding in sales you can achieve all your other goals, for yourself and your family, your level of ambition will increase to the point where you will become absolutely unstoppable. Ambition is a wonderful thing.

NO AMBITION, NO FUTURE

On the other hand, there are people who are not particularly ambitious. Perhaps selling is not the right field for them. In many cases they have achieved a certain level, and they are complacent. They have adjusted their lifestyles to their current incomes and have no real desire to improve them in any way.

Even if you offer them prizes and incentives, they are not motivated enough to work any harder than they already are. These people may be steady, average producers, but they have no real future in the world of competitive selling.

The Conditions of Mediocrity

Not long ago, I was called in to work with a large national company. They wanted me to motivate and stimulate their salespeople with ideas on how to set goals, work more efficiently, and get more done.

Throughout the morning, I gave a high-energy presentation, sharing with them some of the best ideas I had learned with thousands of salespeople in different fields. But it was a ho-hum audience. Most of the people sat leaning back in their chairs, seldom taking notes, occasionally reading the newspaper or conversing with their friends. I had never seen anything like it.

Finally, I asked one of the senior salespeople at the break how things were going. What he told me really opened my eyes. He said that this material was of little interest to him, or to any of the others. All these salespeople were *unionized* and received a fixed hourly rate. The average person had been with the company for twenty years. Nothing they did or didn't do would increase or decrease their income whatsoever. Most of them were "lifers." Their plan was to stay with the company for life, and then retire on a pension.

IMPOSSIBLE TO MOTIVATE

He said, "I can't relate to anything you are saying. I have no ambition. I don't care if I do more or if I do less. It doesn't change my income or my position. It doesn't change my responsibilities either. Why should I work any harder than I am already? I like to just work my eight hours and then go home and watch TV."

This salesman was about forty years old. I thought to myself, *what a tragedy. He will probably live to about eighty, but his fire has already gone out at forty. He has no ambition or desire for anything except an easy job and night-time television.* Lack of ambition is a real waster of time and talent.

Join the Top 20 Percent

One of the most powerful of all time management principles is for you to get better at the most important things you do. You know that 20 percent of the salespeople earn 80 percent of the money. Invariably, the top 20 percent have taken the time and made the investment to become very good at the key things they do. The better you get at what you do, the more money you will make and the sooner you will make it.

Remember, *no one is smarter than you, and no one is better than you.* Everyone starts at the bottom. Everybody who is doing

well today was once doing feebly. And anything that anyone else has learned, you can learn as well. If someone is
doing better than you, it is only because they have learned
the key skills *before* you have. And the proof that you can
learn those skills is that *they* have learned those skills, starting from nothing and not knowing them in the first place.

Start Early, Stay Later

Schedule your first appointment early. Often, the people
who are the hardest to get to are the ones who *can* see you
at seven or seven thirty in the morning. Sometimes they
come in even earlier.

I have found over the years that the best time to see key
decision makers is before and after normal working hours.
This is especially true with successful entrepreneurs and
company owners. The reason they are at the top is because
they start earlier and work later. If you stretch your selling
day and arrange to see them at times that are convenient for
them, you can often make the best sales of your career.

The people who are the *hardest* to get to see usually turn
out to be the most valuable customers. The ones who have
all the time in the world seldom buy anything.

Apply the 80/20 Rule to Everything

Practice the 80/20 rule in everything you do. Spend 80
percent of your time prospecting until you have so much

business that you don't have time to see anyone else. Then spend 80 percent of your time on the 20 percent of prospects that can account for 80 percent of your business, those customers who buy the most from you.

Make a Game of Seeing People

Like a runner at the mark, when the starting gun goes off at eight o'clock on Monday morning, you get going as hard and as fast as you can. All day, every sales day, make it a game to get in front of as many people as you possibly can.

You might even play this game in competition with one of your friends at work. Each of you set a goal to call on 100 prospects as quickly as possible. See my section on the 100-Call Method in chapter 1.

Here's what will happen. By the time you finish calling on 100 prospects, you will be positive, optimistic, enthusiastic, and more than anything else, extremely knowledgeable about your product or service. You will have no fears of rejection or failure left at all. You will have heard every single possible comment and question that you will ever get from a customer. You will know how to sell at a higher level than ever before.

Make Every Minute Count

Think in terms of *minutes* rather than hours. Make every minute count. Move *faster* in everything you do. Pick up the pace. Develop a *sense of urgency* and a bias for action. Move quickly.

When you get in to the office, don't wait until the coffee is ready. Get to work. And when you start work, work *all the time* you work. Don't drop off your dry cleaning, pick up your laundry, or go shopping. Work every minute and every hour.

> *The best time to see key decision makers is before and after normal working hours. This is especially true with successful entrepreneurs and company owners. The reason they are at the top is because they start earlier and work later.*

Make a decision to earn the reputation as the hardest-working person in your company. Don't tell anyone about your decision. Just make sure that, when anyone looks at you, you are working full blast. You don't take breaks or waste time. As far as you're concerned, this is not playtime. It is work time.

If someone says, "Have you got a minute to talk?" say, "Sure, but not right now. Right now I have to get *back to work!*"

COFFEE BREAKS CAN MAKE YOU RICH

Don't waste coffee breaks. When people go to college or start their first jobs, much of their day is built around coffee breaks and lunch. When they arrive in the morning, they start thinking about when they are going to take their coffee break and begin organizing the people with whom they will take that break. But this is not for you.

Since you only get paid for *results*, don't do anything that doesn't pay. Instead, save the time that average people take in coffee breaks and use it to increase your sales. This can have a remarkable effect on your income, and far faster than you realize.

AN IMMEDIATE PAY INCREASE

The average person takes two coffee breaks per day at about 20 minutes each, and sometimes longer, if no one is watching. That is 40 minutes per day. These 40 minutes, times five days per week, equal 200 minutes per week; 200 minutes per week times 50 weeks per year is *10,000 minutes*. That is the equivalent of 166 hours of working time, or more than one full month of additional pay that you give up by taking coffee breaks.

> *When you resolve to spend every coffee break doing something productive, you very quickly add one month's salary to your income.*

When you resolve to spend every coffee break doing something productive, you very quickly add one month's salary to your income. That one-month difference in pay can be equal to buying yourself a new home, a new car, a vacation, or even retiring five years earlier than the average person.

BOOST YOUR INCOME

Make your lunchtime count. The average person, going back to college and his first job, takes an hour for lunch each day. One hour a day equals five hours per week. When you multiply five hours times 50 working weeks a year, it comes out to 250 hours. That's equal to more than six weeks of working time, wasted in an activity that contributes nothing to your life.

By combining coffee breaks and lunches, and using that time to make more sales, you can quickly add two and a half months to your working year, or an income increase of almost 25 percent, from the first day. Since everything you do repeatedly becomes a habit, *effectiveness* will also soon be a habit. You will *habitually* use your time well. You will develop the *habit* of earning more than anyone else around you. These are excellent habits for you to have.

Learn All You Can

Attend sales seminars regularly. Before a sales seminar becomes publicly available, it has been tested and proven with hundreds and even thousands of professionals in that field. The person presenting the seminar has often invested hundreds of hours in research and thousands of hours of experience to bring this seminar together.

When you attend a seminar, you will learn some of the very best ideas ever discovered in that field. Attending seminars can save you weeks, months, and even years of hard work. I have met sales professionals who have doubled and tripled their incomes in as little as thirty days from one idea that they got at one seminar.

Put the Odds in Your Favor

The law of probabilities largely explains success and failure. Successful people *do more things* that are likely to lead them to success. Unsuccessful people do fewer things. By the law of probabilities, successful people are much more likely to do the right thing at the right time in the right way than unsuccessful people.

When you attend sales seminars on a regular basis, you dramatically increase the probability that you will learn what you need to learn to achieve the goals you have set for yourself. This doesn't mean that every idea will be relevant to you at the moment. But if you get enough different ideas, by the law of probabilities, you will almost inevitably get the one or two ideas that can change your career for the better.

This is why the top 10 percent of professionals in every field attend sales seminars. I give seminars all over the United States and Canada, and in twenty-three other countries. Without exception, the highest-paid, most successful sales professionals in the industry are at those seminars. The low-income earners are sitting back at the office worrying about money and complaining about how tough business is. But the top people are aggressively learning everything they possibly can to increase their sales and their incomes.

We've already discussed the merits of reading in your field and taking advantage of the condensed knowledge to be discovered on audio programs. Now imagine that you read one hour per day, attend sales seminars regularly, and listen to audio programs in your car. Suddenly you can make one additional sale per day! Once you have developed the habit of making one additional sale per day, you will automatically move up to *two* additional sales per day, and so on.

What kind of an impact would that have on your results and your income? Think about it! You can become one of the most competent and well-paid professionals in your industry by continuing to upgrade your skills as a part of your daily life.

Manage Your Time Well

Peter Drucker once wrote, "Action without thinking is the cause of every failure." One of the most powerful ways for you to increase your sales and your income is to engage in advance planning.

The more time you take to think through and plan your sales activities, the more effective you will be and the more sales you will make.

Use a time management system. Any time management system will help you as long as you use it as a natural extension of your business activities. You can use a paper time planner, a Palm Pilot, a BlackBerry, or anything else.

It always takes a little time to learn how to incorporate a new time management system into your life. But this investment in time will pay off. At a minimum, you will add two hours of productive time to your day just by using a time planner to organize your day. As you become more fluent with a time planner and with time management, you will double your productivity, your performance, and your income.

Increase Your Earning Ability

You are your most important asset, your most precious resource. Your time is the only thing that you have to sell. And your hourly rate is the key measure of how well you are using yourself. It is the best measure of how effectively you are applying your talents and skills to your life and to your world.

Your *earning ability* is your most valuable financial asset. Everything you do to increase your earning ability enhances the quality of your life.

Return on Energy

When I conduct strategic planning sessions for corporations, we concentrate on improving the measure of *return on equity*. This is the return to the owners of the company on the actual amount of money invested in the business. It is the chief measure for strategic planning and business effectiveness.

In your life, however, your primary equity is *mental, emotional,* and *physical*. In your personal strategic planning, you concentrate on increasing your *return on energy*. Concentrate on increasing your hourly rate and on the results that you get out of every minute of every day.

Self-Made Millionaires

In their book *The Millionaire Next Door*, Thomas Stanley and William Danko found that 79 percent of self-made millionaires in America were entrepreneurs and salespeople. It turned out that the most important skill for success in entrepreneurship was *the ability to sell a product or service.* Sales skills opened almost every door.

By the law of probabilities, your ability to sell well moves you to the front of the line in terms of financial potential. The probability of your achieving financial independence, and even becoming a millionaire, is higher as the result of being better in sales than in any other field. And there are no limits to what you can accomplish except the ones in your *own mind.*

Action Exercises:

1. Resolve today to double both your productivity and your income; calculate your current *hourly rate* and multiply it by two.

2. Plan every day in advance; make a list of everything you have to do, and then set priorities on your list; always start with your number one task.

3. Start each day by asking yourself, *what can I, and only I, do that, if done well, will make the greatest difference in my work?*

4. Upgrade your skills continually; always ask yourself, *what one skill, if I developed and did it in an excellent manner, would help me the most to double my income?* Whatever your answer, work on that skill every day.

5. Develop a sense of urgency, a bias for action; get up and get going early. Work all the time you work.

6. Read sixty minutes each morning, attend sales seminars four times per year, and listen to audio learning programs in your car; never stop getting better.

7. Analyze your sales activities daily; determine exactly how many prospects you will have to see to make a certain number of sales and earn a certain level of income; then raise the bar on yourself. Be the best!

....

Anything that is wasted effort represents wasted time. The best management of our time thus becomes inseparably linked with the best utilization of our efforts.

—Alec MacKenzie

....

CONCLUSION

THIS IS THE BEST TIME IN HISTORY TO BE ALIVE. MORE wealth is being created in more ways, all over the world, than ever before.

Millions of new businesses are started each year, all of them dependent for success on the salespeople who sell their products and services. Almost all the wealth being created today starts with someone selling something to someone else. You are, therefore, at the front of the line for higher income and financial independence.

Perhaps the most important single success principle ever discovered is *learn from the experts*. You will never live long enough to figure it all out for yourself by living trial and error. The good news is that all the answers have already been found. Whatever you want to accomplish, especially in selling, has already been achieved thousands, if not millions, of times. And what others have done, you can do as well.

Perhaps the most outwardly identifiable quality of successful salespeople is *action-orientation*. They learn about a new method or technique and they try it out immediately. When you try a new way or making or closing a sale, only two things can happen: success or failure. If you succeed, you keep on doing it, getting better and better in the process.

If you fail, if the new technique doesn't work, you can try it again, learn from it, and become smarter and more competent. But you can't lose!

When I began selling, I made a decision that changed my life. I resolved that I would try a new method or technique five or ten times before I gave up on it. I later learned that nothing works the first time. The development of key skills takes lots of practice. Like learning to ride a bicycle, you fall down a few times before you master the skill. But after learning, you can do it easily and naturally for the rest of your life.

In the same way, all sales skills are *learnable*. You can learn any sales skill, including closing skills, that you need to achieve any sales goal you can set for yourself. There are no limits.

Your job now is to take those practical, proven methods, techniques, and strategies and apply them over and over—until you become one of the greatest sales professionals of your generation.

Go for it!
Brian Tracy

About the Author

Brian Tracy is one of America's leading authorities on the development of human potential and personal effectiveness. He's a dynamic and entertaining speaker with a wonderful ability to inform and inspire audiences toward peak performance and high levels of achievement.

He addresses more than 250,000 men and women each year on the subjects of personal and professional development, including the executives and staff of IBM, PepsiCo, Ford, Federal Express, Northwestern Mutual, and The Million Dollar Round Table. His exciting talks and seminars on leadership, sales, management, and personal success bring about immediate changes and long-term results.

Brian has a B. Comm. and an MBA, and is the chairman of Brian Tracy International, a human resource company based in San Diego, California, with affiliates throughout America and in 31 other countries worldwide.

Prior to founding Brian Tracy International, Brian was the Chief Operating Officer of a development company with $265 million in assets. He has had successful careers in sales and marketing, investments, real estate development and syndication, importation, distribution, and management consulting. He has conducted high-level consulting assignments with several billion-dollar-plus corporations in strategic planning and organizational development.

Brian has traveled and worked in over 90 countries on six continents, and he speaks four languages. He is an avid reader in management, psychology, economics, metaphysics, and history, and he brings a unique perspective and style to his talks. He has the remarkable ability to capture and hold audience attention with a fast-moving combination of stories, examples, humor, and concrete, practical ideas that get results—fast.

Brian is the author of more than 40 books, including *The Psychology of Selling*, *Be a Sales Superstar*, *Maximum Achievement*, *Advanced Selling Strategies*, *The 100 Absolutely Unbreakable Laws of Business Success*, and *Getting Rich Your Own Way*. He is the author/narrator of more than 300 audio and video training programs, including *The Psychology of Achievement*, *Breaking the Success Barrier*, *The Psychology of Selling*, *Peak Performance Woman*, *Million Dollar Habits*, *The Science of Self-Confidence*, *Thinking Big*, and *How to Master Your Time*.

Brian is married with four children and lives in Solana Beach, California. He is active in community affairs and works closely with nonprofit organizations nationwide.

BRIAN TRACY'S FOCAL POINT ADVANCED COACHING AND MENTORING PROGRAM

THIS INTENSIVE ONE-YEAR PROGRAM IS IDEAL FOR AMBItious, successful entrepreneurs and sales professionals who want to achieve better results and greater balance in their lives.

If you are already earning more than $100,000 per year and you have a large degree of control over your time, in four full days with Brian Tracy in San Diego, one day every three months, you will learn how to double your productivity and income, and double your time off with your family at the same time.

Every 90 days, you will work with Brian Tracy and with an elite group of successful entrepreneurs, self-employed professionals, and top salespeople for an entire day. During this time together, you will form a "mastermind alliance" from which you gain ideas and insights that you can apply immediately to your work and personal life.

The Focal Point process is based on four areas of effectiveness: *Clarification, Simplification, Maximization,* and *Multiplication.* You will learn a series of methods and strategies to incorporate these principles into everything you do.

CLARIFICATION

You will learn how to develop absolute clarity about who you *really* are and what you really want in each of seven key areas of life. You will determine your values, vision, mission, purpose, and goals for yourself, your family, and your work.

SIMPLIFICATION

You will learn how to dramatically simplify your life, getting rid of all the little tasks and activities that contribute little to the achievement of your real goals of high income, excellent family relationships, superb health and fitness, and financial independence. You will also learn how to streamline, delegate, outsource, minimize, and eliminate all those pursuits that are of little value.

MAXIMIZATION

You will learn how to get the very most out of yourself by implementing the best time and personal management tools and techniques ever discovered. You will be taught how to get more done in less time, increase your income rapidly, and have even more time for your personal life.

MULTIPLICATION

You will learn how to leverage your special strengths to accomplish vastly more than you could by relying on your own efforts and resources. You'll learn how to use other people's *money*, other people's *efforts*, other people's *ideas*, and other people's *customers and contacts* to increase your personal productivity and earn more money.

BRIAN TRACY GIVES THIS PROGRAM PERSONALLY FOUR times each year in San Diego. Each session includes complete prework, detailed exercises, and instruction, plus meals and refreshments during the day, and all materials. At the end of each session, you will emerge with a complete blueprint for the next 90 days.

If you are interested in attending this program, visit our Web site at briantracy.com, or phone our vice president, Gary Kewish, at 1-800-542-4252, ext. 18, to request more information or an application. We look forward to hearing from you.